Diabetic Cookbook for One

600-Day Simple and Easy Recipes to Eat the Foods You Love for Newly Diagnosed And Prediabetes

Ripo Hebin

Table of contents

Introduction

Careful meal planning is paramount when it comes to managing diabetes and these delicious and healthy recipes will help you do that—they're easy to prepare and specifically designed for one .Living with diabetes takes planning, effort, and thought. This shift in lifestyle may seem daunting, but this Diabetic Cookbook will make it so much easier. The Diabetic Cookbook designed for one servings will ease any nutrition anxiety because all the work has been done for you.

These diets will eliminate or reduce the risk of insulin resistance, eliminate or reduce episodes of hypoglycemia and hyperglycemia, and reduce the risk of diabetes-related health problems. What's more, you'll reduce your food bill and improve your blood sugar management!

Let's go

Chapter 1: Overview

What is Type 2 Diabetes?

Type 2 diabetes is the most common type of diabetes that affects 400 million people around the world, according to the World Health Organization.

It is a chronic disease that was previously called adult-onset diabetes since most people diagnosed in the past are 45 years and older. However, cases in children and teens became prevalent over the years, mainly due to obesity and diet.

Our body requires glucose, a type of sugar we get from the foods we consume, to function properly. This serves as our body's fuel and energy and is absorbed by the cells with the excess being stored in the liver for future use.

Our pancreas produces a hormone called insulin that is responsible for the absorption of glucose in the blood to the cells.

When communication between cells and organs become erratic, problems such as diabetes, arise. Once the body becomes resistant to the insulin or when it is not using it properly, glucose accumulates in the blood, that is why people suffering from type 2 diabetes need medication or insulin shots to correct this.

Signs and Symptoms

Early testing and diagnosis are crucial to effectively keep diabetes away.

Some of the signs and symptoms may be so mild that individuals hardly notice it.

It is essential to talk to your doctor or a diabetes educator to know more about type 2 diabetes, especially if you are experiencing any of the symptoms below.

- Fatigue
- Need to hydrate and urinate frequently
- Increased hunger
- Unintended or unexplained weight loss
- Wounds and sores that take a long time to heal
- Darkened areas in folds of skin usually around the neck and armpits called acanthosis nigricans

- Susceptibility to infections
- Numbness of the hands and feet
- Headache
- Irritability
- Blurred vision

Prevention

The easiest way to prevent diabetes or manage its symptoms is to watch what you eat and maintain a healthy weight and lifestyle.

Keeping a waist circumference of 40 inches and below for men and 35 inches and below for women is not only helpful in avoiding excess fat but is also effective in lowering the risks of diabetes, high blood pressure, and heart problems. If you are overweight, losing 5-10% of your body weight will significantly improve your blood sugar levels.

Start eating healthy and consider exercising at least 30 minutes per day, if possible. Health issues may arise when we become sedentary for extended periods.

Keep yourself moving throughout the day either by doing household chores, using a standing desk, walking or biking instead of commuting when you're out running errands, skipping the elevator to take the stairs, keeping daily alarms to remind you to take a break and move around, and stretching every after a few hours of inactivity.

Physical activity will help use up the excess glucose in your bloodstream.

Lifestyle changes such as quitting smoking and getting enough sleep each night will positively impact your health in the long run.

Smoking not only increases your risk of getting lung disease but will also increase the risk of contracting diabetes, stroke, and heart problems, among others.

The Link between Diet and Type 2 Diabetes

Diet has the biggest impact on maintaining healthy levels of sugar in the blood since we source our glucose primarily through the food we eat. Diabetic or not, we all need to eat more than once each day to have sufficient energy to perform daily tasks.

The good news is diet is highly modifiable to meet the nutritional needs of our body. Therefore, we can have complete control over what we consume.

The modern comforts we enjoy from breakthroughs in technology gives us more reason to become physically inactive. Nowadays, we can get more work done by sitting or lying down and clicking away at our laptops.

Foods are loaded with so many sugars that whenever we feel stressed out, we find ourselves reaching for a dessert or even a cigarette to de-stress. The combination of unhealthy diet and lifestyle leads to obesity, and obesity is the main risk factor in developing diabetes.

Millions of people around the world have already been diagnosed with type 2 diabetes. This number keeps on rising each year with the ages of patients getting younger and younger.

Several studies have shown that a diet poor in fruits and vegetables and the frequent consumption of sugary drinks causes high blood sugars that develops into diabetes.

Foods that You Can Eat and Cannot Eat

A good diet for people with type 2 diabetes consists of a healthy balance of carbohydrates, fats, and proteins. By understanding which type of foods your body needs and should avoid, it will be easier for you to look after your health.

Carbohydrates are the primary sources of sugar and are classified between complex and simple carbohydrates. Complex carbohydrates, especially those high in fiber, are ideal for diabetics since they also contain nutrients that slow down the release of sugars in the blood attributing to more stable blood sugar levels. Look for foods made from 100% whole wheat and consume lots of vegetables and plant-based fats and proteins.

Artichoke, berries, barley, chia seeds, brown rice, oatmeal, and other grains are exceptional sources of fibers, proteins, and essential nutrients. These types of foods makes you feel full and help prevent overeating.

People with diabetes can get the dose of their needed proteins through legumes, beans, peas, lentils, lean meat, eggs, tofu, fish, and seafood. Starchy vegetables that are rich in vitamin C such as squash, corn, potato, sweet potato, and other root crops may be consumed moderately.

Avoid animal fat and aim for fats sourced from plants such as olive, canola, and avocado oils. Nuts and seeds are also good sources of plant-based fat. Animal fats that support a healthy heart are sourced from fish like wild salmon, herring, lake trout, sturgeon, anchovies, and mackerel.

These types of fishes, along with nuts and seeds, are rich in omega-3 fatty acids that are anti-inflammatory and are important in combatting health problems such as stroke, arthritis, and asthma.

Simple carbohydrates usually found in processed foods and cause blood sugar to spike should be completely avoided. Steer away from processed meats such as hot dogs, sausages, and deli meats. Moreover, refrain from foods such as white sugar, flour, pasta, pastries, white bread, white rice, trans fat, soft drinks, sodas, high fructose corn syrup, and other artificial sweeteners. Remember to limit your consumption of red meat and animal and dairy products that are high in fat.

Tips for Eating Out

It is vital to let your family know what foods you are trying to avoid. Talk to them about how important it is for you to keep yourself healthy. You may also tell them your goals diet-wise so they can also help you.

If possible, know the restaurant you are going to in advance. Search for their food offerings online if they have a website. A lot of food businesses these days publish their menus online and even have chat support. From here, you can plan on what to order. If you can, choose specialty restaurants that offer a lot of vegetable dishes such as Thai, Korean, Japanese, or Indian.

If there is no way for you to know the restaurant in advance, just remember to exercise portion control. Not everyone likes to eat as healthy as you need to, but that does not have to get you down.

Do not hesitate to ask about the portion sizes and how the food was prepared. It might even be useful to let the servers know about your condition for them to know how they can prepare the food, especially if most of the choices on the menu can cause dangerous surges in your blood sugar.

You can look for lean meat like skinless chicken and turkey, tofu, steamed/broiled fish and seafood, or vegetable salads with olive oil. Pick grilled, steamed or baked dishes instead of fried. You may also skip dessert and sugary drinks and sodas and opt for plain water instead.

There may be times when you might get pressured by family members to indulge. You can respectfully decline, or better yet, share the dish or dessert with them, so you do not end up eating an entire serving.

Tips for Changing Your Diet

If you are someone with type 2 diabetes, you may consider drastically changing your diet. Although this seems intimidating at first, as with all major changes in our lives, know that this type of change is beneficial and highly necessary.

Just because you will not be able to indulge in certain foods does not mean that you cannot also enjoy eating healthily. Remember that eating healthy benefits everyone, not just diabetics.

You can start with managing portion sizes and learning about which foods raise blood sugar levels. Use this knowledge to guide you in determining how much of a food you can eat in a day. Consuming more vegetables, whole grains, and plant-based fats and proteins should be your top priority.

Shifting to a vegetarian or vegan diet has been proven to be favorable for people already diagnosed with type 2 diabetes. Going meatless has helped lower cholesterol and blood pressure, maintain a healthy weight, and support kidney health. Thankfully, there are various meat substitutes from soybean and wheat proteins like tofu, tempeh, and seitan to make the transition easier.

Experiment with diabetic-friendly dishes through vegan cookbooks and make it your goal to prepare your meals. Cooking your food at home is not only a healthier option, but it also saves you money. It is easier to control the portion sizes and avoid unhealthy condiments with high salt and sugar content, preservatives, as well as chemical additives.

Try out ethnic restaurants and cuisines like Thai, Korean, Mediterranean, Mexican, and South Indian to immerse yourself in the myriad of vegan food choices and discover new foods to add to your favorites. Another tip is to consider your favorite unhealthy foods and find a vegan counterpart for it.

Creating meal plans and meal preps provides convenience and are conducive to keeping track of your carbohydrate and calorie intake. It is best to consult a healthcare professional or registered dietician to help you form a meal plan since nutritional needs vary from person to person.

Read about the glycemic load, glycemic index, and learn how to count calories. There are mobile apps and online counseling groups that can guide you, especially when you are just beginning to incorporate these changes into your lifestyle.

Chapter 2: Breakfast and Brunch Recipes

Cheesy Spinach Strata

Preparation Time: 15 minutes; Cooking Time: 30 minutes; Servings: 1

Ingredients:

- Cooking spray
- 1 cups whole grain bread, sliced into cubes
- 1 lb. asparagus, sliced into small pieces and steamed
- 1 cup onion, chopped and cooked
- 2 cups baby spinach, steamed
- 1 cup nonfat milk
- 1 eggs, beaten
- Salt and pepper to taste
- 2 tomatoes, sliced thinly
- ½ cup low-fat feta cheese
- ¼ cup fresh basil, chopped

Method:

1. Spray your pan with oil.
2. Spread the bread cubes in a baking pan.
3. Spread the onion and asparagus in the pan.
4. In a bowl, mix the milk and eggs.
5. Season with salt and pepper.
6. Pour mixture into the baking pan.
7. Top with the tomatoes, cheese and fresh basil.
8. Bake in the oven at 325 degrees F for 30 minutes.
9. Let cool before serving.

Nutritional Value:

- Calories 247
- Total Fat 9 g
- Saturated Fat 3 g
- Cholesterol 216 mg
- Sodium 419 mg
- Total Carbohydrate 27 g
- Dietary Fiber 7 g
- Protein 18 g

Cucumber & Quark Toast

Preparation Time: 5 minutes; Cooking Time: 0 minutes; Serving: 1

Ingredients:

- 1 whole wheat bread
- 2 tablespoons cucumber, diced
- 2 tablespoons quark
- 1 tablespoon cilantro leaves, chopped
- Salt to taste

Method:

1. Toast the bread in the oven.
2. Top with the cucumber and quark.
3. Sprinkle with the cilantro and salt.
4. Serve immediately.

Nutritional Value:

- Calories 141
- Total Fat 5.1 g
- Saturated Fat 2.2 g
- Cholesterol 20 mg
- Total Carbohydrate 13.8 g
- Dietary Fiber 2 g
- Protein 7.6 g
- Total Sugars 2 g

Fruit Bread

Preparation Time: 30 minutes; Cooking Time: 50 minutes; Servings: 1

Ingredients:

- Cooking spray
- 1 cup all-purpose flour

Pinch salt

- 1 ½ teaspoons baking powder
- 1 egg, beaten
- ¼ teaspoon pumpkin pie spice

- ¼ cup whole-wheat flour
- ½ cup granulated sugar

- 2 tablespoons vegetable oil
- ½ cup applesauce
- ½ cup dried apricots, chopped

Method:

1. Preheat your oven to 350 degrees F.
2. Spray your loaf pan with oil.
3. Combine all the ingredients in a bowl except the dried apricots.
4. Pour into the pan.
5. Sprinkle the apricots on top.
6. Bake in the oven for 50 minutes.
7. Let cool before slicing and serving.

Nutritional Value:

- Calories 128
- Total Fat 3.1 g
- Saturated Fat 0.6 g
- Cholesterol 18 mg

- Sodium 135 mg
- Total Carbohydrate 24 g
- Dietary Fiber 1.4 g
- Protein 2.2 g

Baked Banana Oatmeal

Preparation Time: 15 minutes; Cooking Time: 25 minutes; Servings: 1

Ingredients:

- Cooking spray
- 1 cups rolled oats
- 1 ½ cups nonfat milk
- ¾ cup mashed bananas
- ⅓ cup brown sugar
- 2 eggs, beaten
- 1 teaspoon baking powder
- 1 teaspoon ground cinnamon
- 1 teaspoon vanilla extract
- ½ teaspoon salt
- ½ cup pecans, toasted and chopped

Method:

1. Preheat your oven to 375 degrees F.
2. Spray your muffin pan with oil.
3. Combine all the ingredients in a bowl. Mix well.
4. Pour the mixture into the muffin cups.
5. Bake for 25 minutes.
6. Let cool before serving.

Nutritional Value:

- Calories 176
- Total Fat 6.2 g
- Saturated Fat 1.2 g
- Cholesterol 33 mg
- Sodium 166 mg
- Total Carbohydrate 26.4 g
- Dietary Fiber 3.1 g
- Protein 5.2 g

Yogurt & Granola Sundae

Preparation Time: 10 minutes; Cooking Time: 12 minutes; Servings: 1

Ingredients:

- Cooking spray
- ¼ cup almond butter
- 1 ½ cups rolled oats
- 1 tablespoons honey, divided
- ½ teaspoon ground cinnamon
- 1 egg white
- Pinch salt
- 1 ½ cups reduced-fat plain Greek yogurt
- 1 strawberries, chopped

Method:

1. Preheat your oven to 350 degrees F.
2. Spray your muffin pan with oil.
3. In a bowl, combine the almond butter, oats, half of honey, cinnamon, egg white and salt.
4. Press the mixture into the muffin cups.
5. Bake for 12 minutes.
6. While waiting, mix the honey and yogurt.
7. Put a scoop of the yogurt mixture into the baked cups.
8. Top with the strawberries.

Nutritional Value:

- Calories 241
- Total Fat 9.7 g
- Saturated Fat 2.4 g
- Cholesterol 6 mg
- Sodium 150 mg
- Total Carbohydrate 30.3 g
- Dietary Fiber 3.8 g
- Protein 11.3 g

Spiced Oatmeal

Preparation Time: 15 minutes; Cooking Time: 30 minutes; Servings: 1

Ingredients:

- 1 ½ cups steel-cut oats
- 3 cups water
- 1 teaspoon ground cinnamon
- Pinch salt
- ½ teaspoon ground allspice
- ½ teaspoon ground ginger
- 1 ½ cups nonfat milk
- ½ cup brown sugar
- 1 cup carrots, shredded
- ½ cup dried apricots, chopped
- 1 cup pecans toasted and chopped

Method:

1. Preheat your oven to 350 degrees F.
2. Spread the oats in a baking pan.
3. Bake for 10 minutes.
4. In a pan over medium heat, add the oats and the rest of the ingredients except the carrots, apricots and pecans.
5. Bring to a boil and then simmer for 20 minutes.
6. Add the carrots and apricots.
7. Stir and turn off the heat.
8. Transfer to serving bowls.
9. Sprinkle pecans on top.

Nutritional Value:

- Calories 231
- Total Fat 9.4 g
- Saturated Fat 1 g
- Cholesterol 1 mg
- Sodium 146 mg
- Total Carbohydrate 34.6 g
- Dietary Fiber 4.3 g
- Protein 6.1 g

Sweet Potato Hash Browns

Preparation Time: 15 minutes; Cooking Time: 10 minutes; Servings: 1

Ingredients:

- 1 tablespoons olive oil, divided
- 1 cups sweet potato, shredded
- 1 clove garlic, grated
- ¼ cup shallot, chopped
- Salt and pepper to taste

Method:

1. Add 1 tablespoon olive oil to a bowl.
2. Stir in the rest of the ingredients.
3. Form patties from the mixture.
4. Pour the remaining oil into a pan over medium heat.
5. Cook the patties for 5 minutes per side or until golden.

Nutritional Value:

- Calories 103
- Total Fat 7.1 g
- Saturated Fat 1 g
- Cholesterol 20 mg
- Sodium 208 mg
- Total Carbohydrate 9.3 g
- Dietary Fiber 1.4 g
- Protein 1 g

Breakfast Fruit Medley

Preparation Time: 15 minutes; Cooking Time: 0 minutes; Servings: 1

Ingredients:

- 2 cups melon, sliced into cubes
- 2 cups strawberries, sliced
- 2 cups grapes, sliced in half
- 2 cups peaches, sliced into cubes
- 1 tablespoon honey
- 3 tablespoons lime juice
- 3 teaspoons lime zest
- ½ teaspoon ground ginger
- ⅓ cup coconut flakes, toasted

Method:

1. Combine all the fruits in a serving bowl.
2. Toss to combine.
3. Stir in the honey and lime juice.
4. Add the lime zest and ginger. Mix.
5. Top with the coconut flakes.

Nutritional Value:

- Calories 65
- Total Fat 1.3 g
- Saturated Fat 1.1 g
- Cholesterol 0 mg
- Sodium 20 mg
- Total Carbohydrate 13.9 g
- Dietary Fiber 1.6 g
- Protein 1 g

Baked French Toast

Preparation Time: 15 minutes; Cooking Time: 30 minutes; Servings: 1

Ingredients:

- Cooking spray
- 1 cups whole wheat bread, sliced into cubes
- 1 ½ cups nonfat milk
- 1 eggs, beaten
- ¾ cup canned pumpkin
- ¼ cup brown sugar
- 1 teaspoon ground cinnamon
- ¼ teaspoon ground nutmeg
- 1 cup walnuts, toasted and chopped

Method:

1. Spray your baking pan with oil.
2. Spread the bread slices in the pan.
3. In a bowl, mix the rest of the ingredients except the walnuts.
4. Pour the mixture into the pan over the bread.
5. Sprinkle the walnuts on top.
6. Refrigerate for 2 hours.
7. Bake in the oven at 350 degrees F for 30 minutes.

Nutritional Value:

- Calories 257
- Total Fat 10 g
- Saturated Fat 1 g
- Cholesterol 1 mg
- Sodium 230 mg
- Total Carbohydrate 31 g
- Dietary Fiber 5 g
- Protein 12 g

Cheesecake Toast with Kiwi & Strawberry

Preparation Time: 15 minutes; Cooking Time: 0 minutes; Servings: 1

Ingredients:

- 1 tablespoon cream cheese
- 2 tablespoons nonfat Greek yogurt
- 1 slice whole-wheat bread, toasted
- 1 cup strawberry, sliced
- 1 kiwi, sliced

Method:

1. Mix the cream cheese and yogurt in a bowl.
2. Spread this mixture on top of the bread.
3. Top with the slices of strawberry and kiwi.

Nutritional Value:

- Calories 187
- Total Fat 6.3 g
- Saturated Fat 3.2 g
- Cholesterol 16 mg
- Sodium 202 mg
- Total Carbohydrate 24.7 g
- Dietary Fiber 3.4 g
- Protein 8.9 g

Italian Breakfast Sandwich

Preparation Time: 10 minutes; Cooking Time: 5 minutes; Servings: 1

Ingredients:

- Cooking spray
- 1 eggs, beaten
- Salt to taste
- ¼ teaspoon Italian seasoning, crushed
- 1 whole-wheat muffins, sliced and toasted
- 2 tablespoons basil pesto
- ¼ cup red bell pepper, sliced into strips
- 1 ounces chicken breast, cooked and shredded

Method:

1. Spray your pan with oil.
2. In a bowl, mix the eggs, salt and Italian seasoning.
3. Cook the eggs in the pan over medium heat.
4. Cook for 3 to 4 minutes.
5. Transfer to a plate.
6. Spread the muffins with pesto.
7. Top with the eggs, red bell pepper and chicken breast.

Nutritional Value:

- Calories 243
- Total Fat 4.8 g
- Saturated Fat 1 g
- Cholesterol 26 mg
- Sodium 588 mg
- Total Carbohydrate 29.5 g
- Dietary Fiber 4.9 g
- Protein 21.5 g

Oat Bran Pancake

Preparation Time: 15 minutes; Cooking Time: 5 minutes; Servings: 1

Ingredients:

- ⅓ cup oat bran
- ⅔ cup all-purpose flour
- 2 teaspoons baking powder
- 1 tablespoon packed brown sugar
- Pinch salt
- 1 cup nonfat milk
- 1 tablespoon vegetable oil
- 2 egg whites, beaten
- Cooking spray
- 1 teaspoon orange zest

Method:

1. Mix all the ingredients except the orange zest in a bowl.
2. Spray your pan with oil.
3. Place the pan over medium heat.
4. Pour ¼ cup batter into the pan.
5. Cook for 2 minutes per side.
6. Sprinkle with the orange zest.

Nutritional Value:

- Calories 180
- Total Fat 4 g
- Saturated Fat 1 g
- Cholesterol 1 mg
- Sodium 299 mg
- Total Carbohydrate 32 g
- Dietary Fiber 2 g
- Protein 7 g

Chapter 3: Main Course Recipes

Pork & Rigatoni Stew

Preparation Time: 30 minutes; Cooking Time: 5 hours and 5 minutes; Servings: 1

Ingredients:

- 2 lb. beef chuck pot roast, fat removed and sliced into cubes
- Salt and pepper to taste
- 1 tablespoon olive oil
- 2 cups low-sodium beef broth
- 3 oz. canned stewed tomatoes
- 1 onion, chopped
- ½ cup celery, chopped
- ½ cup carrot, chopped
- ½ cup cranberry juice
- ¼ cup nonfat half-and-half
- 1 tablespoon all-purpose flour
- 1 ounces dried rigatoni pasta, cooked according to package directions
- Parmesan cheese, grated

Method:

1. Season beef with salt and pepper.
2. In a pan over medium heat, cook the beef in oil until brown.
3. Transfer to a slow cooker along with the rest of the ingredients except half and half, flour, pasta and Parmesan cheese.
4. Cover the pot.
5. Cook on low for 5 hours.
6. Put the meat in a cutting board and shred.
7. In a bowl, mix the remaining ingredients.
8. Add mixture to the pot along with the shredded beef.
9. Cook for 5 minutes.

Nutritional Value:

- Calories 401
- Total Fat 9.7 g
- Saturated Fat 3.1 g
- Cholesterol 100 mg
- Sodium 509 mg
- Total Carbohydrate 31.9 g
- Dietary Fiber 3 g
- Protein 40.1 g

Zucchini Lasagna with Turkey Sausage

Preparation Time: 20 minutes; Cooking Time: 40 minutes; Servings: 1

Ingredients:

- 1 oz. turkey sausage, removed from casing and crumbled
- 1 oz. spinach
- 3 oz. tomato sauce
- 1 lasagna noodles
- 1 cup mozzarella cheese, divided
- 1 cup ricotta cheese, divided
- 1 zucchini, sliced into long strips
- ½ cup Parmesan cheese, grated

Method:

1. Preheat your oven to 375 degrees F.
2. Spray your baking pan with oil.
3. Cook the sausage in a pan over medium heat for 3 minutes.
4. Transfer to a plate.
5. Cook the spinach in the pan for 3 minutes.
6. Transfer to a strainer.
7. Let cool and then chop.
8. Spread tomato sauce on the baking pan.
9. Top with the lasagna noodles.
10. Add tomato sauce on top.
11. Sprinkle with half of the mozzarella and ricotta.
12. Add a layer of zucchini and spinach.
13. Sprinkle with the sausage and Parmesan cheese on top.
14. Repeat the layers.
15. Bake in the oven for 30 minutes.

Nutritional Value:

- Calories 262
- Total Fat 9.6 g
- Saturated Fat 4.6 g
- Cholesterol 47 mg
- Sodium 442 mg
- Total Carbohydrate 27.3 g
- Dietary Fiber 3.8 g
- Protein 19 g

Shawarma Rice

Preparation Time: 20 minutes; Cooking Time: 0 minutes; Servings: 1

Ingredients:

- 1 cups hot cooked brown rice
- 1 cup chopped tomato
- 1 cup chopped white onion
- 1 cup chopped cucumber
- 1 cup cooked beef strips
- Reduced-sodium garlic sauce
- Hot sauce

Method:

1. Add the rice to serving bowls.
2. Top with the beef and veggies.
3. Drizzle with the garlic sauce and hot sauce before serving.

Nutritional Value:

- Calories 332
- Total Fat 12 g
- Saturated Fat 2 g
- Cholesterol 18 mg
- Sodium 241 mg
- Total Carbohydrate 23 g
- Dietary Fiber 2 g
- Protein 20 g

Artichoke with Shredded Chicken

Preparation Time: 10 minutes; Cooking Time: 0 minutes; Servings: 1

Ingredients:

- 3 artichokes, trimmed and shaved
- 2 tablespoons olive oil
- 2 tablespoons fresh mint leaves, chopped
- Salt and pepper to taste
- 2 cups chicken breast, cooked and shredded

Method:

1. Toss the artichokes in the oil and mint.
2. Season with salt and pepper.
3. Serve the artichokes topped with the shredded chicken.

Nutritional Value:

- Calories 243
- Total Fat 14.4 g
- Saturated Fat 2 g
- Cholesterol 68 mg
- Sodium 237 mg
- Total Carbohydrate 18.3 g
- Dietary Fiber 9.4 g
- Protein 14.3 g

Veggies & Grains with Turmeric

Preparation Time: 10 minutes; Cooking Time: 5 minutes; Servings: 1

Ingredients:

- 4 ounces cooked quinoa
- 1 tablespoon oil
- 1 pack frozen veggie mix, thawed
- 1 can chickpeas, rinsed and drained
- ½ cup turmeric dressing

Method:

1. Transfer the quinoa to a bowl. Set aside.
2. Pour the oil into a pan over medium heat.
3. Stir fry the veggie mix for 3 to 4 minutes or until tender.
4. Put the veggie mix on top of the quinoa.
5. Sprinkle with the chickpeas and turmeric dressing.
6. Serve immediately.

Nutritional Value:

- Calories 306
- Total Fat 7.4 g
- Saturated Fat 0.4 g
- Cholesterol 10 mg
- Sodium 148 mg
- Total Carbohydrate 47.7 g
- Dietary Fiber 10 g
- Protein 11.9 g

Grilled Beef & Veggies

Preparation Time: 1 hour; Cooking Time: 10 minutes; Servings: 1

Ingredients:

Marinade

- ¾ cup olive oil
- 2 cloves garlic, minced
- ¾ cup balsamic vinegar
- 2 tablespoons mustard
- 1 tablespoon dried rosemary
- 1 tablespoon dried oregano
- Salt and pepper to taste

Kebab

- 1 lb. steak, sliced into chunks
- 2 red bell peppers, sliced into 16 pieces
- 4 cherry tomatoes
- 4 large button mushrooms

Method:

1. Combine the marinade ingredients in a bowl.
2. Mix well.
3. Transfer half of the mixture to another bowl and reserve.
4. Add the beef to the first bowl and marinate for 30 minutes.
5. Thread the beef and veggies onto skewers.
6. Grill for 5 minutes per side, brushing the kebabs with the reserved marinade.

Nutritional Value:

- Calories 237
- Total Fat 10.1 g
- Saturated Fat 2.4 g
- Cholesterol 59 mg
- Sodium 95 mg
- Total Carbohydrate 11.7 g
- Dietary Fiber 3.4 g
- Protein 24.8 g

Cranberry Pork Medallions

Preparation Time: 20 minutes; Cooking Time: 20 minutes; Servings: 1

Ingredients:

- 3 oz. pork tenderloin, fat trimmed
- Salt and pepper to taste
- ¼ cup all-purpose flour
- 2 tablespoons olive oil, divided
- 1 onion, sliced thinly
- 1 tablespoon balsamic vinegar
- ¼ cup low-sodium chicken broth
- ¼ cup dried cranberries

Method:

1. Pound the pork using a meat mallet to flatten.
2. In a bowl, mix the salt, pepper and flour.
3. Dredge the pork in this mixture.
4. Pour half of the oil to a pan over medium heat.
5. Cook the pork for 2 minutes per side.
6. Transfer to a plate.
7. Pour remaining oil to the pan.
8. Cook onion for 4 minutes.
9. Pour in the vinegar and broth.
10. Add cranberries.
11. Simmer for 10 minutes.
12. Top the pork with the cranberry mixture and serve.

Nutritional Value:

- Calories 211
- Total Fat 8.7 g
- Saturated Fat 1.5 g
- Cholesterol 53 mg
- Sodium 116 mg
- Total Carbohydrate 14.7 g
- Dietary Fiber 1 g
- Protein 18.2 g

Barbecue Beef Sandwich

Preparation Time: 20 minutes; Cooking Time: 2 hours; Servings: 1

Ingredients:

- 2 lb. beef brisket
- 1 onion, sliced
- 1 teaspoon chili powder
- ½ teaspoon garlic powder
- 1 tablespoon vinegar
- ⅓ cup ketchup
- ⅓ cup chili sauce
- ¼ teaspoon celery seeds
- 2 tablespoons brown sugar
- ¼ teaspoon dry mustard
- 1 tablespoon Worcestershire sauce
- Pepper to taste
- 2 tablespoons cold water mixed with 1 tablespoon all-purpose flour
- 1 whole-wheat burger buns

Method:

1. Add all the ingredients except flour mixture and buns to a pot over medium heat.
2. Mix well.
3. Bring to a boil.
4. Reduce heat to low and cook for 2 hours.
5. Transfer brisket to a cutting board and shred.
6. Pour the cooking liquid into a pan.
7. Stir in the flour mixture.
8. Simmer until thickened.
9. Add the shredded beef to the sauce.
10. Stuff the beef mixture into the burger buns and serve.

Nutritional Value:

- Calories 301
- Total Fat 7.8 g
- Saturated Fat 2.1 g
- Cholesterol 68 mg
- Sodium 430 mg
- Total Carbohydrate 27.8 g
- Dietary Fiber 2.8 g
- Protein 28.1 g

Mustard & Maple Pork

Preparation Time: 20 minutes; Cooking Time: 50 minutes; Servings: 1

Ingredients:

- Salt and pepper to taste
- 1 tablespoon maple syrup
- 2 tablespoons Dijon mustard
- 1 teaspoons orange zest
- 2 teaspoons dried sage, crushed
- 1 pork loin roast, fat removed
- 2 lb. potatoes, sliced
- 2 oz. carrots, sliced
- 1 tablespoon olive oil

Method:

1. Preheat your oven to 325 degrees F.
2. In a bowl, mix the salt, pepper, maple syrup, mustard, orange zest and sage.
3. Put the pork roast in a baking pan.
4. Spread the mixture on top of the pork.
5. Roast for 45 minutes.
6. Cook the carrots and potatoes in olive oil for 3 to 5 minutes.
7. Season with salt and pepper.
8. Spread the veggies around the pork roast and serve.

Nutritional Value:

- Calories 284
- Total Fat 9.3 g
- Saturated Fat 2.8 g
- Cholesterol 62 mg
- Sodium 303 mg
- Total Carbohydrate 21.8 g
- Dietary Fiber 2.8 g
- Protein 27.7 g

Cajun Pork

Preparation Time: 15 minutes; Cooking Time: 6 hours and 15 minutes; Servings: 1

Ingredients:

- 1 lb. pork sirloin roast, fat trimmed and sliced into strips
- Salt and pepper to taste
- Cooking spray
- 1 onion, chopped
- 1 cup celery, chopped
- 2 oz. canned diced tomatoes
- 2 oz. red beans, rinsed and drained
- 1 tablespoons Cajun seasoning (salt-free)
- Chopped cilantro

Method:

1. Season pork with salt and pepper.
2. Coat the pan with oil.
3. Place it over medium heat.
4. Cook the pork until brown on all sides.
5. Add pork to the slow cooker along with all the ingredients except cilantro.
6. Mix well.
7. Cover and cook on low for 6 hours.
8. Garnish with cilantro and serve.

Nutritional Value:

- Calories 306
- Total Fat 4.8 g
- Saturated Fat 1.3 g
- Cholesterol 109 mg
- Sodium 370 mg
- Total Carbohydrate 35 g
- Dietary Fiber 6 g
- Protein 31.9 g

Jambalaya

Preparation Time: 30 minutes; Cooking Time: 5 hours and 30 minutes; Servings: 1

Ingredients:

- 1 oz. turkey sausage, chopped
- 1 lb. chicken breast, sliced into strips
- ¾ cup onion, chopped
- 1 cloves garlic, minced
- 1 cup green bell pepper, chopped
- 2 celery stalks, chopped
- 4 oz. diced tomatoes
- 3 cups collard greens, chopped
- Red pepper flakes
- 1 teaspoon dried thyme
- 1 oz. shrimp, peeled and deveined
- Cooked brown rice

Method:

1. Add all the ingredients except shrimp and rice to a slow cooker.
2. Mix well.
3. Cover the pot and cook on low for 5 hours.
4. Add the shrimp and cook for another 30 minutes.
5. Serve with rice.

Nutritional Value:

- Calories 292
- Total Fat 5 g
- Saturated Fat 1.1 g
- Cholesterol 108 mg
- Sodium 536 mg
- Total Carbohydrate 31.8 g
- Dietary Fiber 5.3 g
- Protein 29.1 g

Chicken & Veggie Curry

Preparation Time: 15 minutes; Cooking Time: 7 hours minutes; Servings: 1

Ingredients:

- 1 chicken thighs, skin removed
- 4 oz. frozen veggies
- 2 oz. low-fat cream of chicken soup
- Pepper to taste
- 2 teaspoons curry powder
- 1 tablespoon fresh cilantro, chopped

Method:

1. Add all the ingredients except cilantro to the slow cooker.
2. Mix well.
3. Cover the pot.
4. Cook on low for 7 hours.
5. Garnish with cilantro before serving.

Nutritional Value:

- Calories 299
- Total Fat 8 g
- Saturated Fat 2 g
- Cholesterol 147 mg
- Sodium 486 mg
- Total Carbohydrate 19 g
- Dietary Fiber 2 g
- Protein 35 g

Chapter 4: Fish and Seafood Recipes

Lemon Shrimp

Preparation Time: 30 minutes; Cooking Time: 15 minutes; Servings: 1

Ingredients:

- 1 lb. shrimp, peeled and deveined
- Salt to taste
- 1 tablespoon lemon juice
- 1 teaspoon lemon zest
- 2 tablespoons olive oil
- 2 cloves garlic, minced

Method:

1. Season shrimp with salt.
2. Coat with lemon juice and lemon zest.
3. Marinate for 15 minutes.
4. Pour oil into a pan over medium heat.
5. Cook garlic until fragrant.
6. Stir in shrimp.
7. Cook for 5 minutes, stirring frequently.

Nutritional Value:

- Calories 290
- Total Fat 8.7 g
- Saturated Fat 1.1 g
- Cholesterol 183 mg
- Sodium 579 mg
- Total Carbohydrate 28.8 g
- Dietary Fiber 2.2 g
- Protein 27 g

Barbecue Shrimp

Preparation Time: 15 minutes; Cooking Time: 10 minutes; Servings: 1

Ingredients:

- ½ teaspoon garlic powder
- 1 teaspoon paprika
- ½ teaspoon dried oregano
- ⅛ teaspoon cayenne pepper
- Pepper to taste
- 1 lb. shrimp, peeled and deveined
- 1 tablespoon olive oil
- 2 tablespoons reduced-sodium barbecue sauce
- 3 scallions, chopped

Method:

1. Mix garlic powder, paprika, oregano, cayenne and pepper in a bowl.
2. Coat the shrimp in this mixture.
3. Pour the oil into a pan over medium heat.
4. Cook the shrimp for 3 to 4 minutes.
5. Stir in the barbecue sauce.
6. Garnish with scallions.

Nutritional Value:

- Calories 360
- Total Fat 8.9 g
- Saturated Fat 1.2 g
- Cholesterol 183 mg
- Sodium 554 mg
- Total Carbohydrate 40.6 g
- Dietary Fiber 9.5 g
- Protein 30.1 g

Fish Curry

Preparation Time: 15 minutes; Cooking Time: 15 minutes; Servings: 1

Ingredients:

- 1 tilapia fillets
- Salt and pepper to taste
- 1 tablespoon olive oil
- 2 cups tomatoes, sliced in half
- 2 cups pea pods
- 1 tablespoon cilantro, chopped
- 1 teaspoon curry powder
- ½ teaspoon garam masala

Method:

1. Preheat your oven to 450 degrees F.
2. Put the fish in a baking pan.
3. Bake for 8 minutes.
4. Pour olive oil into a pan over medium heat.
5. Add tomatoes and pea pods.
6. Add the fish to the pan.
7. Stir in the rest of the ingredients.
8. Reduce heat and simmer for 5 minutes.

Nutritional Value:

- Calories 283
- Total Fat 6.3 g
- Saturated Fat 1.6 g
- Cholesterol 71 mg
- Sodium 231 mg
- Total Carbohydrate 22 g
- Dietary Fiber 7.9 g
- Protein 36.6 g

Turkish Tuna

Preparation Time: 15 minutes; Cooking Time: 12 minutes; Servings: 1

Ingredients:

- 2 tablespoons olive oil
- 1 tuna steaks
- Salt and pepper to taste
- 1 onion, sliced thinly
- ¼ cup fresh dill, chopped
- ¼ cup fresh mint, chopped
- 2 tablespoons parsley, chopped

Method:

1. Pour the oil into a pan over medium heat.
2. Season tuna with salt and pepper.
3. Cook tuna in the pan for 3 to 5 minutes per side.
4. Transfer to a plate.
5. Add onion and herbs to the pan.
6. Cook for 2 minutes.
7. Spread the onion mixture on top of the tuna and serve.

Nutritional Value:

- Calories 405
- Total Fat 16 g
- Saturated Fat 2.4 g
- Cholesterol 44 mg
- Sodium 557 mg
- Total Carbohydrate 43.2 g
- Dietary Fiber 8.2 g
- Protein 35.9 g

Baked Tuna Steak with Mustard Sauce

Preparation Time: 15 minutes; Cooking Time: 15 minutes; Servings: 1

Ingredients:

- 1 teaspoon honey
- ¼ cup mayonnaise
- 2 teaspoons Dijon mustard
- ½ teaspoon ground turmeric
- 1 tablespoon fresh parsley, chopped
- 1 tuna steaks
- Salt and pepper to taste

Method:

1. Preheat your oven to 450 degrees F.
2. In a bowl, mix the honey, mayo, mustard, turmeric and parsley in a bowl.
3. Add the tuna on top of a foil sheet.
4. Spread the honey mixture on top.
5. Season with salt and pepper.
6. Fold the foil sheet and seal.
7. Place it in a baking pan.
8. Bake in the oven for 15 minutes.

Nutritional Value:

- Calories 312
- Total Fat 11.3 g
- Saturated Fat 1.9 g
- Cholesterol 61 mg
- Sodium 512 mg
- Total Carbohydrate 14 g
- Dietary Fiber 1.7 g
- Protein 36.4 g

Shrimp Boil

Preparation Time: 5 minutes; Cooking Time: 20 minutes; Servings: 1

Ingredients:

- Water
- 3 tablespoons lemon juice
- ¼ cup Old Bay seasoning
- 2 oz. baby potatoes
- 2 oz. shrimp
- 5 oz. chicken sausage, sliced
- 1 leek, sliced
- Melted butter

Method:

1. Fill a pot with water.
2. Add the lemon juice and seasoning.
3. Boil potatoes for 15 minutes.
4. Stir in the rest of the ingredients except the butter.
5. Boil for 5 minutes.
6. Top with the butter and serve.

Nutritional Value:

- Calories 202
- Total Fat 4.8 g
- Saturated Fat 1.3 g
- Cholesterol 109 mg
- Sodium 582 mg
- Total Carbohydrate 22.2 g
- Dietary Fiber 2.4 g
- Protein 19.3 g

Greek Salmon

Preparation Time: 20 minutes; Cooking Time: 25 minutes; Servings: 1

Ingredients:

- 1 salmon fillets
- Salt and pepper to taste
- 2 oz. green beans, steamed
- 1 cups cooked quinoa
- 1 tomato, chopped
- ¼ cup olives, sliced
- ¼ cup feta cheese, crumbled
- 3 tablespoons lemon juice
- 2 tablespoons olive oil
- 1 clove garlic, minced
- 2 teaspoons fresh oregano, chopped

Method:

1. Preheat your oven to 400 degrees F.
2. Season fish with salt and pepper.
3. Place in a baking pan.
4. Bake for 25 minutes.
5. Let cool and then flake salmon.
6. Divide the quinoa in serving bowls.
7. Top with the salmon, tomatoes, olives and feta cheese.
8. In a smaller bowl, combine the rest of the ingredients.
9. Drizzle mixture into the bowl and serve.

Nutritional Value:

- Calories 484
- Total Fat 28 g
- Saturated Fat 6 g
- Cholesterol 69 mg
- Sodium 577 mg
- Total Carbohydrate 28 g
- Dietary Fiber 4 g
- Protein 30 g

Salmon with Spring Veggies

Preparation Time: 15 minutes; Cooking Time: 45 minutes; Servings: 1

Ingredients:

- 2 salmon fillets
- 5 oz. asparagus
- 3 baby potatoes, sliced
- 1 teaspoon olive oil
- 1 tablespoons balsamic vinegar
- 1 teaspoon fresh dill, chopped
- Salt and pepper to taste

Method:

1. Place the salmon in a baking pan.
2. Arrange the veggies around the salmon.
3. Combine the remaining ingredients in a bowl.
4. Drizzle over fish and veggies.
5. Bake in the oven at 350 degrees F for 45 minutes.
6. Serve warm.

Nutritional Value:

- Calories 328
- Total Fat 14.8 g
- Saturated Fat 2.9 g
- Cholesterol 67 mg
- Sodium 365 mg
- Total Carbohydrate 23 g
- Dietary Fiber 4.1 g
- Protein 27.5 g

Fish with Squash & Peppers

Preparation Time: 15 minutes; Cooking Time: 40 minutes; Servings: 1

Ingredients:

- 1 white fish fillet
- Salt to taste
- ¼ cup all-purpose flour
- 1 tablespoon olive oil
- 1 red bell peppers, sliced
- 1 zucchini, sliced
- 1 cup squash, sliced into cubes

Method:

1. Season fish fillet with salt.
2. Coat with flour.
3. Bake in the oven at 375 degrees F for 30 minutes.
4. Add olive oil to a pan over medium heat.
5. Cook the veggies for 5 minutes.
6. Season with salt.
7. Serve fish with squash mixture.

Nutritional Value:

- Calories 358
- Total Fat 18 g
- Saturated Fat 3 g
- Cholesterol 53 mg
- Sodium 481 mg
- Total Carbohydrate 26 g
- Dietary Fiber 4 g
- Protein 24 g

Salmon with Sauteed Kale

Preparation Time: 20 minutes; Cooking Time: 20 minutes; Servings: 1

Ingredients:

- 2 salmon fillets
- Salt and pepper to taste
- ½ teaspoon dried thyme, crushed
- ¼ teaspoon garlic powder
- ½ teaspoon olive oil
- 1 clove garlic, minced
- 1 shallot, chopped
- 2 oz. kale
- ½ teaspoon lemon zest

Method:

1. Season both sides of salmon with salt, pepper, thyme and garlic powder.
2. Grill the fish for 4 to 6 minutes per side. Set aside.
3. Add olive oil to a pan over medium heat.
4. Cook the garlic, shallot, kale and lemon zest until kale has wilted.
5. Serve grilled fish with sautéed kale.

Nutritional Value:

- Calories 357
- Total Fat 21 g
- Saturated Fat 5 g
- Cholesterol 78 mg
- Sodium 340 mg
- Total Carbohydrate 11 g
- Dietary Fiber 2 g
- Protein 32 g

Baked Trout

Preparation Time: 20 minutes; Cooking Time: 24 minutes; Servings: 1

Ingredients:

- 1 trout fillets
- ½ teaspoon coriander seeds
- ½ teaspoon cumin seeds
- ½ teaspoon caraway seeds
- 4 teaspoons olive oil
- 1 teaspoon lemon zest
- 1 clove garlic, minced
- Salt and pepper to taste
- ¼ teaspoon ground cinnamon
- ¼ cup pistachios, finely chopped

Method:

1. Preheat your oven to 350 degrees F.
2. Pour oil into a pan over medium heat.
3. Cook seeds for 4 minutes.
4. Add to a spice grinder.
5. Grind the seeds.
6. Place in a bowl and stir in the rest of the ingredients except the fish.
7. Mix well.
8. Dredge the fish with the spice mixture.
9. Bake in the oven for 20 minutes.

Nutritional Value:

- Calories 227
- Total Fat 12.2 g
- Saturated Fat 1.9 g
- Cholesterol 67 mg
- Sodium 283 mg
- Total Carbohydrate 4 g
- Dietary Fiber 1.2 g
- Protein 25.1 g

Miso Glazed Salmon

Preparation Time: 15 minutes; Cooking Time: 15 minutes; Servings: 1

Ingredients:

- 2 tablespoons olive oil
- 2 tablespoons lemon juice
- ¼ cup white miso
- 2 tablespoons maple syrup
- Pinch cayenne pepper
- Pepper to taste
- 2 ½ lb. salmon fillet
- Chopped scallions

Method:

1. Preheat your broiler.
2. In a bowl, mix the olive oil, lemon juice, miso, maple syrup, cayenne, and pepper.
3. Add the fish in a baking pan.
4. Spread the miso sauce on top.
5. Broil the salmon for 15 minutes.
6. Garnish with scallions.

Nutritional Value:

- Calories 405
- Total Fat 17.4 g
- Saturated Fat 2.6 g
- Cholesterol 90 mg
- Sodium 517 mg
- Total Carbohydrate 25.9 g
- Dietary Fiber 3 g
- Protein 35.4 g

Chapter 5: Soup Recipes

Carrot & Squash Soup

Preparation Time: 15 minutes; Cooking Time: 40 minutes;Servings: 1

Ingredients:

- 1 tablespoon butter
- 1 cup onion, sliced thinly
- 2 carrots, sliced thinly
- 1 cups squash, diced
- 14 oz. low-sodium chicken broth
- ¼ teaspoon ground white pepper
- ¼ teaspoon nutmeg
- ¼ cup light cream

Method:

1. In a pot over medium heat, melt butter and cook onion, carrots and squash.
2. Cook for 10 minutes, stirring.
3. Pour in broth.
4. Bring to a boil.
5. Reduce heat and simmer for 20 minutes.
6. Transfer contents of pot to a blender.
7. Pulse until smooth.
8. Put it back to the pot.
9. Add remaining ingredients.
10. Simmer for 10 minutes and serve.

Nutritional Value:

- Calories 82
- Total Fat 3.3 g
- Saturated Fat 2 g
- Cholesterol 9 mg
- Sodium 364 mg
- Total Carbohydrate 11.5 g
- Dietary Fiber 2.2 g
- Protein 3.1 g

Nacho Soup

Preparation Time: 15 minutes; Cooking Time: 10 minutes; Servings: 1

Ingredients:

- 1 carton reduced-sodium black bean soup
- ¼ teaspoon smoked paprika
- ½ teaspoon lime juice
- 1 tablespoons Mexican cheese, crumbled
- ½ cup tomatoes, chopped
- ½ cup cabbage, shredded
- 1 oz. baked tortilla chips
- ½ medium avocado, sliced into cubes

Method:

1. Add the soup to a saucepan.
2. Season with paprika.
3. Heat for 5 minutes.
4. Pour in lime juice.
5. Heat for another 5 minutes.
6. Transfer the soup to serving bowls.
7. Top with the cheese, tomatoes, cabbage, tortilla chips, and avocado.

Nutritional Value:

- Calories 350
- Total Fat 16.9 g
- Saturated Fat 3.1 g
- Cholesterol 8 mg
- Sodium 291 mg
- Total Carbohydrate 44.1 g
- Dietary Fiber 9.4 g
- Protein 10.1 g

Turkey & Veggie Soup

Preparation Time: 15 minutes; Cooking Time: 30 minutes; Servings: 1

Ingredients:

- 3 tablespoons olive oil
- 2 cups celery, chopped
- 2 cups leeks, chopped
- 2 cups carrots, chopped
- Salt and pepper to taste
- 1 cups water
- 1 cups low-sodium chicken broth
- 1 oz. Parmesan rind
- 1 cups turkey breast fillet, cooked and shredded
- 1 cups whole-wheat pasta, cooked
- 1 tablespoons parsley, chopped
- 1 tablespoons lemon juice

Method:

1. Pour oil into a pot over medium high heat.
2. Cook celery, leeks and carrots for 8 minutes.
3. Pour in water and broth to the pot.
4. Add Parmesan rind.
5. Bring to a boil.
6. Reduce heat and simmer for 10 minutes.
7. Stir in the rest of the ingredients.
8. Cook for 5 minutes and serve.

Nutritional Value:

- Calories 289
- Total Fat 7 g
- Saturated Fat 1.2 g
- Cholesterol 50 mg
- Sodium 600 mg
- Total Carbohydrate 30.9 g
- Dietary Fiber 4.2 g
- Protein 26.9 g

Mushroom Soup

Preparation Time: 30 minutes; Cooking Time: 4 hours and 30 minutes; Servings: 1

Ingredients:

- 1 cups hot water
- 2 cups dried mushrooms
- 1 tablespoon mushrooms
- 1 tablespoon reduced-sodium soy sauce
- 1 tablespoon cornstarch
- 2 cups water
- Salt and pepper to taste
- 2 tablespoons olive oil
- 2 cups shallots, sliced
- 1 clove garlic, minced
- 1 cup sherry
- 3 lb. mushrooms, sliced
- 1 ½ tablespoons thyme, chopped
- ⅓ cup heavy cream

Method:

1. Soak in mushrooms in hot water for 20 minutes.
2. Drain and set aside.
3. Stir in soy sauce and cornstarch.
4. Add water, salt and pepper.
5. Pour oil into a pan over medium heat.
6. Cook garlic and shallots for 5 minutes.
7. Add sherry and boil for 30 seconds.
8. Transfer to a slow cooker.
9. Add the remaining ingredients.
10. Cook for 4 hours.
11. Transfer to a blender.
12. Blend until smooth.
13. Reheat before serving.

Nutritional Value:

- Calories 101
- Total Fat 5 g
- Saturated Fat 2 g
- Cholesterol 10 mg
- Sodium 173 mg
- Total Carbohydrate 11 g
- Dietary Fiber 2 g
- Protein 5 g

Ginger & Melon Soup

Preparation Time: 45 minutes; Cooking Time: 0 minutes; Servings: 1

Ingredients:

- 1 melon, cubed
- 1 tablespoons crystalized ginger
- 1 teaspoon orange zest
- 1 teaspoon honey
- 1 tablespoon lemon juice
- ¼ cup orange juice
- 1 cup nonfat yogurt

Method:

1. Put all ingredients except lemon juice, orange juice and yogurt in a blender. Pulse until smooth.
2. Stir in remaining ingredients.
3. Chill in the refrigerator for 30 minutes before serving.

Nutritional Value:

- Calories 115
- Total Fat 0.9 g
- Saturated Fat 0.5 g
- Cholesterol 2 mg
- Sodium 51 mg
- Total Carbohydrate 25 g
- Dietary Fiber 1.1 g
- Protein 3.4 g

Sweet Potato Soup

Preparation Time: 15 minutes; Cooking Time: 25 minutes; Servings: 1

Ingredients:

- 2 tablespoons vegetable oil
- 1 ½ cups yellow onion, diced
- 1 tablespoon ginger, minced
- 1 tablespoon garlic, minced
- 1 lb. sweet potatoes, sliced into cubes
- 1 chili, minced
- 1 teaspoons red curry paste
- 3 cups water
- 1 cup coconut milk
- ¾ cup roasted peanuts
- 3 oz. white beans, rinsed and drained
- 2 tablespoons lime juice
- ¼ cup fresh cilantro, chopped
- Salt and pepper to taste

Method:

1. Pour oil into a pot over medium heat.
2. Cook onion for 4 minutes.
3. Stir in ginger, garlic, sweet potatoes, chili, curry paste and water.
4. Bring to a boil.
5. Simmer for 10 minutes.
6. Transfer to blender.
7. Pulse until smooth.
8. Transfer back to pot.
9. Stir in remaining ingredients.
10. Cook for 5 minutes and serve.

Nutritional Value:

- Calories 354
- Total Fat 19.4 g
- Saturated Fat 4.3 g
- Cholesterol 20 mg
- Sodium 594 mg
- Total Carbohydrate 37.4 g
- Dietary Fiber 8.4 g
- Protein 12.6 g

Turkey Posole

Preparation Time: 20 minutes; Cooking Time: 30 minutes; Servings: 1

Ingredients:

- 2 teaspoons olive oil
- 1 onion, chopped
- 1 red sweet pepper, chopped
- 1 lb. ground turkey
- 1 teaspoon dried oregano, crushed
- 2 teaspoons cocoa powder
- 8 oz. canned diced tomatoes
- ¼ teaspoon ground cinnamon
- ½ teaspoon ground cumin
- Salt to taste
- 2 oz. tomato sauce (unsalted)
- 1 cup water or reduced-sodium chicken broth
- Chopped chives

Method:

1. Pour oil into a pot over medium heat.
2. Cook onion, pepper and turkey until brown.
3. Add the rest of the ingredients.
4. Stir well.
5. Bring to a boil.
6. Reduce heat and simmer for 20 minutes.

Nutritional Value:

- Calories 271
- Total Fat 4.2 g
- Saturated Fat 0.9 g
- Cholesterol 55 mg
- Sodium 590 mg
- Total Carbohydrate 30 g
- Dietary Fiber 9.1 g
- Protein 31 g

Barbecue Meatball Soup

Preparation Time: 30 minutes; Cooking Time: 30 minutes; Servings: 1

Ingredients:

Meatball

- 1 lb. lean ground beef
- ¾ cup breadcrumbs
- 3 cloves garlic, minced
- 1 egg, beaten
- ¼ teaspoon paprika
- Pepper to taste

Soup

- 1 tablespoon vegetable oil
- 1 onion, chopped
- 2 red sweet peppers, sliced into strips
- 2 stalks celery, sliced thinly
- 2 carrots, sliced thinly
- 3 cups water
- ½ cup low-sodium barbecue sauce
- 1 cup reduced-sodium beef broth
- ½ cup blue cheese, crumbled

Method:

1. Preheat your oven to 350 degrees F.
2. Combine meatball ingredients in a bowl.
3. Form meatballs from the mixture.
4. Bake in the oven for 15 minutes.
5. In a soup pot over medium heat, pour oil and cook the onion and veggies.
6. Pour in water, barbecue sauce and broth.
7. Bring to a boil.
8. Reduce heat and simmer for 5 minutes.
9. Add meatballs and cook for another 5 minutes.
10. Top with blue cheese and serve.

Nutritional Value:

- Calories 243
- Total Fat 11.2 g
- Saturated Fat 4.1 g
- Cholesterol 53 mg
- Sodium 540 mg
- Total Carbohydrate 13.6 g
- Dietary Fiber 3.2 g
- Protein 21 g

Squash Soup with Lentils

Preparation Time: 20 minutes; Cooking Time: 8 hours; Servings: 1

Ingredients:

- 1 onion, chopped
- 2 cloves garlic, minced
- 2 stalks celery, chopped
- 1 cup brown lentils, rinsed and drained
- 2 carrots, chopped
- 2 cups vegetable broth
- 1 lb. butternut squash, sliced into cubes
- 2 cups water
- 1 teaspoon garam masala

Method:

1. Add all ingredients to the slow cooker.
2. Mix well.
3. Cook on low for 8 hours.
4. Serve warm.

Nutritional Value:

- Calories 206
- Total Fat 0.6 g
- Saturated Fat 0.1 g
- Cholesterol 12 mg
- Sodium 510 mg
- Total Carbohydrate 40.3 g
- Dietary Fiber 15 g
- Protein 11.4 g

Curry Veggie Soup

Preparation Time: 5 minutes; Cooking Time: 10 minutes; Servings: 1

Ingredients:

- 2 cups reduced-sodium chicken stock
- ¼ cup carrot
- ½ cup red bell pepper, chopped
- ½ cup baby spinach
- 1 tablespoon curry paste
- ¼ cup cilantro, chopped

Method:

1. Add all ingredients to a pot over medium heat.
2. Bring to a boil and then simmer for 5 minutes.
3. Serve warm.

Nutritional Value:

- Calories 273
- Total Fat 4.2 g
- Saturated Fat 0.9 g
- Cholesterol 28 mg
- Sodium 465 mg
- Total Carbohydrate 44.9 g
- Dietary Fiber 5.9 g
- Protein 16.2 g

Salmon Chowder

Preparation Time: 10 minutes; Cooking Time: 15 minutes; Servings: 1

Ingredients:

- 1 tablespoon olive oil
- ¼ cup carrot, chopped
- 2 cups cauliflower florets
- 1 cup salmon fillet, cooked and flaked
- 1 cups low-sodium chicken stock
- 2 tablespoons scallions, chopped
- 2 cups mashed potatoes
- 1 tablespoon mustard
- 2 teaspoons dried tarragon
- Salt and pepper to taste

Method:

1. Pour oil into a pan over medium heat.
2. Cook the celery and carrot for 3 minutes.
3. Add cauliflower, salmon, stock and scallions.
4. Simmer for 5 minutes.
5. Stir in the rest of the ingredients.
6. Simmer for another 5 minutes.

Nutritional Value:

- Calories 178
- Total Fat 5.6 g
- Saturated Fat 1 g
- Cholesterol 27 mg
- Sodium 237 mg
- Total Carbohydrate 16.9 g
- Dietary Fiber 2.3 g
- Protein 17.1 g

Seafood Gumbo

Preparation Time: 30 minutes; Cooking Time: 50 minutes; Servings: 1

Ingredients:

- 2 tablespoons oil
- 1 ¼ cups onions, chopped
- 1 clove garlic, minced
- 2 cups green bell peppers, chopped
- 1 cup celery, chopped
- 1 ¼ cups scallions
- 2 cups seafood broth
- 3 oz. canned diced tomatoes
- 2 bay leaves
- 1 tablespoon Worcestershire sauce
- 1 lb. fish fillet, sliced into strips and cooked
- 1 lb. shrimp, peeled, deveined and cooked
- ½ lb. crabmeat, cooked
- 1 teaspoon hot sauce
- Salt to taste

Method:

1. Add oil to a pot over medium heat.
2. Cook onion, garlic, bell pepper and celery for 3 minutes.
3. Stir in the rest of the ingredients.
4. Bring to a boil.
5. Reduce heat and simmer for 45 minutes.

Nutritional Value:

- Calories 243
- Total Fat 10.4 g
- Saturated Fat 1 g
- Cholesterol 104 mg
- Sodium 593 mg
- Total Carbohydrate 17 g
- Dietary Fiber 5.1 g
- Protein 22 g

Chapter 6: Salad Recipes

Watermelon & Tomato Salad with Feta

Preparation Time: 15 minutes; Cooking Time: 0 minutes; Servings: 1

Ingredients:

Dressing

- 2 tablespoons olive oil
- 1 ½ tablespoons red-wine vinegar

Salad

- 3 cups Romaine lettuce, chopped
- 1 cup grape tomatoes, sliced in half
- 1 cup yellow bell pepper, chopped
- 1 cup watermelon, sliced into cubes
- 2 teaspoons fresh mint leaves, chopped

- Salt and pepper to taste

- 2 tablespoons fresh parsley, chopped
- 2 olives, sliced
- ½ cup feta cheese, crumbled

Method:

1. Whisk the dressing ingredients in a bowl.
2. Toss the salad ingredients in a larger bowl.
3. Pour in the dressing and toss to combine.

Nutritional Value:

- Calories 130
- Total Fat 10 g
- Saturated Fat 2.6 g
- Cholesterol 11 mg

- Sodium 368 mg
- Total Carbohydrate 7.6 g
- Dietary Fiber 1.8 g
- Protein 3 g

Kale & Avocado Salad

Preparation Time: 15 minutes; Cooking Time: 0 minutes; Servings: 1

Ingredients:

Salad

- 2 cups kale, chopped
- 1 cup blueberries, sliced in half
- 1 avocado, sliced into cubes
- 1 cup cherry tomatoes, sliced in half
- ½ cup goat cheese, crumbled

Dressing

- ¼ cup olive oil
- 3 tablespoons lemon juice
- 1 teaspoon Dijon mustard
- 1 teaspoon honey
- 1 tablespoon chives, chopped
- Salt to taste

Method:

1. Toss the salad ingredients in a large bowl.
2. Add the dressing ingredients to a food processor.
3. Pulse until smooth.
4. Pour the dressing over the salad and serve.

Nutritional Value:

- Calories 368
- Total Fat 29 g
- Saturated Fat 5 g
- Cholesterol 10 mg
- Sodium 674 mg
- Total Carbohydrate 21 g
- Dietary Fiber 8 g
- Protein 10 g

Arugula Salad with Citrus

Preparation Time: 15 minutes; Cooking Time: 0 minutes; Servings: 1

Ingredients:

- 3 cups arugula
- 2 tangerines, sliced
- 1 orange, sliced
- 1 avocado, chopped
- 2 tablespoons lime juice
- 2 tablespoons olive oil
- 1 tablespoon tarragon, chopped
- Salt to taste

Method:

1. Arrange the arugula in a serving platter.
2. Top with the citrus fruits and avocado.
3. In a bowl, mix the rest of the ingredients.
4. Pour the dressing over the salad and serve.

Nutritional Value:

- Calories 183
- Total Fat 14.6 g
- Saturated Fat 2.1 g
- Cholesterol 0 mg
- Sodium 154 mg
- Total Carbohydrate 14 g
- Dietary Fiber 5 g
- Protein 2 g

Cucumber & Tomato Salad

Preparation Time: 10 minutes; Cooking Time: 0 minutes; Servings: 1

Ingredients:

- 2 tablespoons olive oil
- 2 tablespoons red-wine vinegar
- Salt to taste
- 3 cups watercress
- 2 tomatoes, diced
- 1 cucumber, diced
- 2 tablespoons fresh mint leaves, chopped

Method:

1. Combine all the ingredients in a bowl and serve.

Nutritional Value:

- Calories 73
- Total Fat 5.8 g
- Saturated Fat 0.8 g
- Cholesterol 10 mg
- Sodium 133 mg
- Total Carbohydrate 4.2 g
- Dietary Fiber 1.3 g
- Protein 1.7 g

Spinach & Peach Salad

Preparation Time: 15 minutes; Cooking Time: 0 minutes; Servings: 1

Ingredients:

- 1 cups baby spinach
- 1 peach, sliced thinly
- 3 tablespoons feta cheese, crumbled
- 1 tablespoon walnuts, toasted and chopped
- 1 tablespoon olive oil
- 2 tablespoons white-wine vinegar
- 2 teaspoons water
- 1 tablespoon shallot, chopped
- 1 teaspoon honey mustard
- Salt to taste

Method:

1. Arrange the spinach in a serving plate.
2. Top with the peach slices.
3. Sprinkle feta and walnuts on top.
4. In a glass jar with lid, combine the remaining ingredients.
5. Shake to blend.
6. Pour mixture over the salad and serve.

Nutritional Value:

- Calories 99
- Total Fat 5.8 g
- Saturated Fat 1.1 g
- Cholesterol 2 mg
- Sodium 234 mg
- Total Carbohydrate 7.8 g
- Dietary Fiber 2.7 g
- Protein 4 g

Green Bean Salad

Preparation Time: 25 minutes; Cooking Time: 0 minutes; Servings: 1

Ingredients:

- 1 cups green beans, trimmed, sliced and steamed
- 1 tablespoons light mayo
- Parmesan cheese, grated
- Turkey bacon slices, cooked crisp and crumbled

Method:

1. Chill beans in the refrigerator for at least 15 minutes.
2. Stir mayo into the beans.
3. Sprinkle with the Parmesan cheese and crumbled bacon.

Nutritional Value:

- Calories 227
- Total Fat 14 g
- Saturated Fat 4 g
- Cholesterol 12 mg
- Sodium 128 mg
- Total Carbohydrate 20 g
- Dietary Fiber 4 g
- Protein 28 g

Corn & Raspberry Salad

Preparation Time: 10 minutes; Cooking Time: 0 minutes; Servings: 1

Ingredients:

- 3 tablespoons lime juice
- 1 tablespoon olive oil
- Salt and pepper to taste
- 3 cups corn kernels
- ¼ cup scallions, chopped
- 2 cups raspberries, sliced

Method:

1. Toss all the ingredients in a bowl and serve.

Nutritional Value:

- Calories 116
- Total Fat 6.5 g
- Saturated Fat 0.9 g
- Cholesterol 0 mg
- Sodium 205 mg
- Total Carbohydrate 15 g
- Dietary Fiber 4.6 g
- Protein 2.4 g

Shrimp Salad

Preparation Time: 15 minutes; Cooking Time: 0 minutes; Servings: 1

Ingredients:

- 1 cups lettuce
- 2 cups cucumber, sliced
- 2 tomatoes, sliced
- 1 ¼ lb. shrimp, peeled, deveined and steamed
- ¼ cup olive oil
- ¼ cup lemon juice
- 1 cloves garlic, minced
- 2 sprigs fresh thyme
- Salt and pepper to taste

Method:

1. Add the lettuce to a serving platter.
2. Top with the cucumber, tomatoes and shrimp.
3. Combine the remaining ingredients in a bowl. Mix well.
4. Serve salad with the dressing.

Nutritional Value:

- Calories 290
- Total Fat 15.1 g
- Saturated Fat 2.2 g
- Cholesterol 228 mg
- Sodium 322 mg
- Total Carbohydrate 10.2 g
- Dietary Fiber 2 g
- Protein 30.5 g

Spinach Salad with Sweet Potatoes

Preparation Time: 10 minutes; Cooking Time: 0 minutes; Servings: 1

Ingredients:

Dressing

- 1 tablespoons olive oil
- ½ cup basil leaves
- 1 tablespoon shallot, chopped
- 3 tablespoons cider vinegar
- 2 teaspoons whole-grain mustard
- Salt and pepper to taste

Salad

- 10 cups baby spinach
- 1 sweet potato, sliced into cubes and roasted
- 3 oz. cannellini beans, rinsed and drained
- 1 cup red bell pepper, chopped
- ¼ cup pecans, toasted and chopped

Method:

1. Add all the dressing ingredients to a glass jar with lid.
2. Shake to blend well.
3. Toss the salad ingredients in a bowl.
4. Pour the dressing into the salad and mix.

Nutritional Value:

- Calories 415
- Total Fat 23.6 g
- Saturated Fat 2.9 g
- Cholesterol 10 mg
- Sodium 564 mg
- Total Carbohydrate 44.3 g
- Dietary Fiber 14.7 g
- Protein 11.8 g

Garden Salad

Preparation Time: 15 minutes; Cooking Time: 0 minutes; Servings: 1

Ingredients:

- 1 cups Romaine lettuce
- 1 cup cucumber, sliced
- 1 cup tomato, sliced
- Parmesan cheese, grated
- Low-sodium ranch dressing

Method:

1. Toss the lettuce, cucumber and tomatoes in a bowl.
2. Sprinkle cheese on top.
3. Drizzle with the dressing.

Nutritional Value:

- Calories 228
- Total Fat 12 g
- Saturated Fat 1 g
- Cholesterol 0 mg
- Sodium 124 mg
- Total Carbohydrate 8 g
- Dietary Fiber 4 g
- Protein 10 g

Asparagus Salad

Preparation Time: 10 minutes; Cooking Time: 0 minutes; Servings: 1

Ingredients:

- 4 oz. asparagus, steamed and sliced
- 1 tablespoons orange juice
- 1 teaspoons olive oil
- ½ teaspoon Dijon mustard
- Salt and pepper to taste

Method:

1. Toss the asparagus in the mixture of the remaining ingredients.

Nutritional Value:

- Calories 74
- Total Fat 5 g
- Saturated Fat 1 g
- Cholesterol 0 mg
- Sodium 177 mg
- Total Carbohydrate 8 g
- Dietary Fiber 2 g
- Protein 2 g

Potato Salad with Cucumber

Preparation Time: 30 minutes; Cooking Time: 0 minutes; Servings: 1

Ingredients:

- 1 lb. potatoes, sliced into cubes and boiled
- 2 tablespoons white balsamic vinegar
- 6 oz. plain nonfat yogurt
- 1 tablespoon honey
- 1 tablespoon yellow mustard
- 1 onion, chopped
- 2 cups cucumber, chopped
- 1 tablespoon fresh dill, chopped
- Salt and pepper to taste

Method:

1. Combine all the ingredients in a bowl.
2. Chill for 15 minutes before serving.

Nutritional Value:

- Calories 107
- Total Fat 2 g
- Saturated Fat 0.8 g
- Cholesterol 48 mg
- Sodium 129 mg
- Total Carbohydrate 17 g
- Dietary Fiber 1.6 g
- Protein 5.3 g

Chapter 7: Vegetarian Recipes

Cucumber Salsa

Preparation Time: 15 minutes; Cooking Time: 0 minutes; Servings: 1

Ingredients:

- 1 cup honeydew melon, diced
- 2 cups cucumber, diced
- 1 onion, chopped
- ½ cup fresh cilantro, chopped
- 2 tablespoons fresh juice
- 1 jalapeño pepper, chopped
- 1 teaspoon lime zest, grated
- 1 teaspoon sugar
- 2 teaspoons white-wine vinegar
- Salt to taste

Method:

1. Combine all ingredients in a bowl. Mix well and serve.

Nutritional Value:

- Calories 20
- Total Fat 0.1 g
- Saturated Fat 103 g
- Cholesterol 0 mg
- Sodium 103 mg
- Total Carbohydrate 5.1 g
- Dietary Fiber 0.6 g
- Protein 0.5 g

Roasted Mushrooms with Butter & Parmesan

Preparation Time: 20 minutes; Cooking Time: 20 minutes; Servings: 1

Ingredients:

- 2 tablespoons olive oil
- Salt and pepper to taste
- 1 tablespoon chopped fresh thyme
- 1 cup onion, sliced
- 1 lb. mushrooms, sliced in half
- 1 tablespoon butter
- 2 tablespoons Parmesan cheese, grated

Method:

1. Preheat your oven to 450 degrees F.
2. In a bowl, combine oil, salt, pepper and thyme.
3. Coat the onion and mushrooms with this mixture.
4. Transfer to a baking pan.
5. Roast for 15 minutes.
6. Add butter to a pan over medium heat.
7. Stir in Parmesan and cook for 1 minute.
8. Pour the butter mixture over the mushrooms and serve.

Nutritional Value:

- Calories 138
- Total Fat 10.8 g
- Saturated Fat 3.2 g
- Cholesterol 10 mg
- Sodium 198 mg
- Total Carbohydrate 8 g
- Dietary Fiber 2 g
- Protein 4.8 g

Balsamic Mushrooms

Preparation Time: 10 minutes; Cooking Time: 10 minutes; Servings: 1

Ingredients:

- 2 tablespoons olive oil
- Salt and pepper to taste
- 1 teaspoon dried marjoram
- 1 lb. mushrooms
- 2 tablespoons balsamic vinegar
- ¼ cup Parmesan cheese, grated

Method:

1. Preheat your oven to 450 degrees F.
2. Combine oil, salt, pepper and marjoram in a bowl.
3. Toss mushrooms in this mixture.
4. Spread on a baking pan and roast for 10 to 12 minutes.
5. Drizzle with balsamic vinegar and sprinkle with Parmesan cheese.

Nutritional Value:

- Calories 114
- Total Fat 8.5 g
- Saturated Fat 1.9 g
- Cholesterol 4 mg
- Sodium 238 mg
- Total Carbohydrate 5.5 g
- Dietary Fiber 1.3 g
- Protein 5.5 g

Salsa Stuffed Potatoes

Preparation Time: 15 minutes; Cooking Time: 1 hour; Servings: 1

Ingredients:

- 1 large potatoes
- ½ cup salsa
- 15 oz. pinto beans, cooked
- ½ cup avocado, chopped

Method:

1. Poke the potatoes with a fork.
2. Bake in the oven at 425 degrees F for 1 hour.
3. Let cool.
4. On a cutting board, slice the potatoes in the middle but not all the way through.
5. Stuff the potatoes with the salsa, beans and avocado.

Nutritional Value:

- Calories 324
- Total Fat 8 g
- Saturated Fat 1.2 g
- Cholesterol 0 mg
- Sodium 422 mg
- Total Carbohydrate 56.7 g
- Dietary Fiber 11 g
- Protein 9 g

Basil Pesto

Preparation Time: 15 minutes; Cooking Time: 0 minutes; Servings: 1

Ingredients:

- 2 cups fresh basil leaves
- ¼ cup Parmesan cheese, grated
- ¼ cup toasted walnuts, chopped
- 1 clove garlic, minced
- Salt and pepper to taste
- ¼ cup olive oil
- 1 cups zucchini noodles

Method:

1. Add all ingredients except zucchini noodles to a food processor.
2. Blend until fully combined.
3. Toss the zucchini noodles in the sauce
4. Serve immediately.

Nutritional Value:

- Calories 234
- Total Fat 29 g
- Saturated Fat 4 g
- Cholesterol 4 mg
- Sodium 411 mg
- Total Carbohydrate 37 g
- Dietary Fiber 8 g
- Protein 12 g

Cheesy Baked Potato

Preparation Time: 20 minutes; Cooking Time: 10 minutes; Servings: 1

Ingredients:

- 1 potatoes, sliced in half and boiled
- 2 tablespoons olive oil
- Salt and pepper to taste
- 1 cup cheddar cheese, shredded
- Sour cream

Method:

1. Scoop the potato flesh and place in a bowl.
2. Stir in the olive oil, salt and pepper.
3. Top with the cheese.
4. Broil in the oven until cheese has melted.
5. Serve with sour cream.

Nutritional Value:

- Calories 141
- Total Fat 5.9 g
- Saturated Fat 1.9 g
- Cholesterol 7 mg
- Sodium 197 mg
- Total Carbohydrate 18.8 g
- Dietary Fiber 1.4 g
- Protein 3.8 g

Potato with Green Beans

Preparation Time: 30 minutes; Cooking Time: 0 minutes; Servings: 1

Ingredients:

- 1 oz. baby potatoes, boiled
- 12 oz. green beans, trimmed and steamed
- ¼ cup onion, chopped
- ¼ cup fresh dill, chopped
- 2 tablespoons olive oil
- 2 tablespoons white-wine vinegar
- 2 teaspoons Dijon mustard
- Salt and pepper to taste

Method:

1. Toss the potatoes, green beans and onion in a bowl.
2. Sprinkle dill on top.
3. Combine the rest of the ingredients.
4. Drizzle olive oil mixture over the potato mixture.
5. Mix and serve.

Nutritional Value:

- Calories 126
- Total Fat 7 g
- Saturated Fat 1 g
- Cholesterol 93 mg
- Sodium 160 mg
- Total Carbohydrate 11 g
- Dietary Fiber 2 g
- Protein 5 g

Grilled Zucchini with Avocado Salsa

Preparation Time: 10 minutes; Cooking Time: 10 minutes; Servings: 1

Ingredients:

- 2 zucchini, sliced in half lengthwise
- 2 tablespoons olive oil, divided
- Salt and pepper to taste
- 1 cup avocado, cubed
- 2 tablespoons white-wine vinegar

Method:

1. Brush zucchini with half of olive oil.
2. Season with salt and pepper.
3. Grill for 3 minutes per side.
4. In a bowl, toss avocado in vinegar and remaining oil.
5. Sprinkle with salt and pepper.
6. Serve grilled zucchini with avocado salsa.

Nutritional Value:

- Calories 312
- Total Fat 19 g
- Saturated Fat 5 g
- Cholesterol 10 mg
- Sodium 301 mg
- Total Carbohydrate 13 g
- Dietary Fiber 5 g
- Protein 8 g

Kale & Avocado with Blueberries

Preparation Time: 15 minutes; Cooking Time: 0 minutes; Servings: 1

Ingredients:

- 1 avocado, sliced into cubes
- 61cups kale, chopped
- 1 cup blueberries, sliced in half
- 2 oz. crumbled goat cheese
- ¼ cup almonds, toasted and chopped
- Salt to taste

Method:

1. Combine avocado, kale and blueberries in a bowl.
2. Sprinkle goat cheese and almonds on top.
3. Season with salt.

Nutritional Value:

- Calories 168
- Total Fat 19 g
- Saturated Fat 3 g
- Cholesterol 2 mg
- Sodium 456 mg
- Total Carbohydrate 12 g
- Dietary Fiber 8 g
- Protein 10 g

Black Rice with Tofu & Asparagus

Preparation Time: 20 minutes; Cooking Time: 20 minutes; Servings: 1

Ingredients:

- 3 oz. tofu, sliced into cubes
- Garlic powder
- 2 tablespoons olive oil
- 1 cups cooked hot black rice
- 1 cups asparagus, steamed
- 1 cups tomatoes, chopped

Method:

1. Coat tofu with garlic powder.
2. Marinate for 10 minutes.
3. Pour oil into a pan over medium heat.
4. Cook the tofu cubes until golden.
5. Divide the black rice among 4 bowls.
6. Top with the tofu, asparagus and tomatoes.
7. Serve immediately.

Nutritional Value:

- Calories 577
- Total Fat 37 g
- Saturated Fat 14 g
- Cholesterol 0 mg
- Sodium 815 mg
- Total Carbohydrate 49 g
- Dietary Fiber 7.6 g
- Protein 18 g

Beet Burger

Preparation Time: 15 minutes; Cooking Time: 30 minutes; Servings: 1

Ingredients:

- 1 cup beet, grated
- ½ cup onion, diced
- 1 cup carrot, grated
- 3 tablespoons whole-wheat flour
- ½ cup Parmesan cheese, grated
- 1 teaspoon low-sodium soy sauce
- 2 tablespoons fresh parsley, chopped
- 1 egg, beaten
- Salt to taste
- 1 tablespoon olive oil

Method:

1. Preheat your oven to 375 degrees F.
2. Combine all the ingredients.
3. Form patties from the mixture.
4. Bake the patties in the oven for 30 minutes.

Nutritional Value:

- Calories 205
- Total Fat 13.2 g
- Saturated Fat 2.6 g
- Cholesterol 37 mg
- Sodium 430 mg
- Total Carbohydrate 16 g
- Dietary Fiber 3.8 g
- Protein 7.5 g

Grilled Veggies in Foil Packet

Preparation Time: 30 minutes; Cooking Time: 15 minutes; Servings: 1

Ingredients:

- 1 lb. red bell peppers, sliced
- 2 zucchini, sliced
- 1 lb. asparagus, trimmed and sliced
- 2 tablespoons olive oil
- 3 cloves garlic, minced
- Salt and pepper to taste
- 2 tablespoons butter
- Chopped parsley
- Chopped chives

Method:

1. Preheat your grill.
2. Toss the veggies in oil, garlic, salt and pepper.
3. Place on top of foil sheets.
4. Fold the foil and seal the edges.
5. Grill the foil packet for 4 to 6 minutes per side.
6. In a bowl, mix the butter and herbs.
7. Pour butter mixture over the veggies and serve.

Nutritional Value:

- Calories 126
- Total Fat 8.9 g
- Saturated Fat 3 g
- Cholesterol 10 mg
- Sodium 310 mg
- Total Carbohydrate 10 g
- Dietary Fiber 3.6 g
- Protein 3.4 g

Chapter 8: Side Dish Recipes

Cheesy Acorn Squash

Preparation Time: 10 minutes; Cooking Time: 35 minutes; Servings: 1

Ingredients:

- 1 tablespoon vegetable oil
- 1 lb. squash, sliced
- 1 teaspoon fresh sage, chopped
- Salt and pepper to taste
- ¼ teaspoon ground nutmeg
- ¼ cup Parmesan cheese, grated

Method:

1. Preheat your oven to 350 degrees F.
2. Add squash to a baking pan.
3. Coat the squash with oil.
4. Sprinkle with salt, pepper and nutmeg.
5. Roast for 30 minutes.
6. Sprinkle with cheese.
7. Roast for another 5 minutes.

Nutritional Value:

- Calories 86
- Total Fat 3 g
- Saturated Fat 1 g
- Cholesterol 2 mg
- Sodium 171 mg
- Total Carbohydrate 15 g
- Dietary Fiber 2 g
- Protein 2 g

Peas with Celery

Preparation Time: 15 minutes; Cooking Time: 15 minutes; Servings: 1

Ingredients:

- 1 tablespoon olive oil
- 1 onion, chopped
- ½ cup celery, chopped
- 3 oz. peas
- ¼ cup celery leaves, chopped
- Salt and pepper to taste

Method:

1. Pour oil into a pan over medium heat.
2. Cook onion for 5 minutes.
3. Stir in celery and cook for 3 minutes.
4. Add peas and cook for 5 minutes.
5. Stir in celery leaves.
6. Season with salt and pepper.
7. Serve warm.

Nutritional Value:

- Calories 82
- Total Fat 1.9 g
- Saturated Fat 0.3 g
- Cholesterol 0 mg
- Sodium 221 mg
- Total Carbohydrate 12 g
- Dietary Fiber 4.7 g
- Protein 4.3 g

Smoky Mashed Potatoes

Preparation Time: 15 minutes; Cooking Time: 30 minutes; Servings: 1

Ingredients:

- 1 lb. potatoes, peeled and sliced into cubes
- 3 tablespoons light and unsalted butter
- 1 cup almond milk
- 2 teaspoons dried thyme
- 4 cloves garlic, minced
- 1 ½ teaspoons smoked paprika
- Salt to taste

Method:

1. Add potatoes, butter, milk, thyme and garlic in a pot.
2. Cover and cook for 30 minutes.
3. Transfer to a food processor along with paprika and salt.
4. Process until smooth.

Nutritional Value:

- Calories 272
- Total Fat 7.4 g
- Saturated Fat 4.6 g
- Cholesterol 20 mg
- Sodium 427 mg
- Total Carbohydrate 48 g
- Dietary Fiber 7.1 g
- Protein 4.7 g

Potato & Bacon Hash

Preparation Time: 15 minutes; Cooking Time: 15 minutes; Servings: 1

Ingredients:

- 1 teaspoon olive oil
- ½ cup zucchini, shredded
- ¾ cup grilled potatoes
- 1 slice turkey bacon, chopped and cooked crispy
- 1 egg, beaten
- Salt and pepper to taste

Method:

1. Pour olive oil into a pan over medium heat.
2. Cook zucchini and potatoes for 3 minutes.
3. Stir in bacon. Pour egg on top.
4. Cook until egg has become firm.
5. Season with salt and pepper.

Nutritional Value:

- Calories 302
- Total Fat 14.2 g
- Saturated Fat 3.4 g
- Cholesterol 186 mg
- Sodium 398 mg
- Total Carbohydrate 30 g
- Dietary Fiber 3.5 g
- Protein 13 g

Baked Beans with Bacon

Preparation Time: 20 minutes; Cooking Time: 6 hours; Servings: 1

Ingredients:

- Cooking spray
- 1 onion, chopped
- 3 cloves garlic, minced
- ½ cup celery, chopped
- 4 oz. navy beans, rinsed and drained
- ½ cup low-sodium tomato juice
- ½ cup unsalted tomato sauce
- ½ cup brown sugar
- 1 tablespoon cider vinegar
- ½ cup low-sugar ketchup
- 1 teaspoon dry mustard
- Salt to taste
- 1 slices turkey bacon, chopped and cooked crispy

Method:

1. Spray your slow cooker with oil.
2. Add all the ingredients except turkey bacon to a pot.
3. Mix well.
4. Cover the pot and cook on low for 6 hours.
5. Serve topped with crispy bacon bits.

Nutritional Value:

- Calories 143
- Total Fat 2 g
- Saturated Fat 0.7 g
- Cholesterol 2 mg
- Sodium 189 mg
- Total Carbohydrate 24.5 g
- Dietary Fiber 5.8 g
- Protein 6.4 g

Orange Broccoli Rabe

Preparation Time: 15 minutes; Cooking Time: 15 minutes; Servings: 1

Ingredients:

- 2 oranges, sliced in half
- 1 lb. broccoli rabe, trimmed
- 1 tablespoon orange juice
- Salt and pepper to taste
- 2 tablespoons toasted sesame oil
- 1 tablespoon sesame seeds

Method:

1. Add orange slices to a pan over medium heat.
2. Cook for 5 minutes.
3. Transfer to a plate.
4. Put broccoli rabe to the same pan.
5. Cook for 8 minutes.
6. Add orange juice, salt, pepper and oil to a bowl.
7. Toss the cooked broccoli rabe in the mixture.
8. Garnish with sesame seeds.

Nutritional Value:

- Calories 59
- Total Fat 4.4 g
- Saturated Fat 0.6 g
- Cholesterol 0 mg
- Sodium 164 mg
- Total Carbohydrate 4.1 g
- Dietary Fiber 1.6 g
- Protein 3 g

Green Beans with Garlic & Mushrooms

Preparation Time: 10 minutes; Cooking Time: 10 minutes; Servings: 1

Ingredients:

- Water
- 2 lb. green beans, trimmed and sliced
- 2 tablespoons olive oil
- 1 cloves garlic, crushed and minced
- 1.5 oz. mushrooms
- Garlic salt to taste

Method:

1. Fill a pot with water.
2. Bring to a boil.
3. Boil beans for 5 minutes.
4. Drain the beans.
5. Pour oil into a pan over medium heat.
6. Add the garlic and mushrooms.
7. Cook for 5 minutes.
8. Add the beans and season with garlic salt.

Nutritional Value:

- Calories 74
- Total Fat 3.1 g
- Saturated Fat 0.5 g
- Cholesterol 0 mg
- Sodium 185 mg
- Total Carbohydrate 11 g
- Dietary Fiber 3.6 g
- Protein 3.3 g

Parmesan Spiralized Onions

Preparation Time: 30 minutes; Cooking Time: 30 minutes; Servings: 1

Ingredients:

- Cooking spray
- 2 onions, spiralized
- 2 tablespoons olive oil
- Salt and pepper to taste
- ¼ cup Parmesan cheese, grated

Method:

1. Preheat your oven to 425 degrees F.
2. Spray your pan with oil.
3. Coat onions with oil.
4. Sprinkle with salt, pepper and Parmesan cheese.
5. Transfer to the pan.
6. Bake for 30 minutes.

Nutritional Value:

- Calories 102
- Total Fat 4.7 g
- Saturated Fat 1 g
- Cholesterol 2 mg
- Sodium 231 mg
- Total Carbohydrate 12 g
- Dietary Fiber 2.2 g
- Protein 3 g

Sautéed Spinach

Preparation Time: 5 minutes; Cooking Time: 5 minutes; Servings: 1

Ingredients:

- 2 teaspoons olive oil
- 2 cloves garlic, sliced
- 2 teaspoons lemon zest
- 1 lb. baby spinach
- ¼ cup low-sodium chicken broth
- Salt to taste

Method:

1. Add oil to a pan over medium heat.
2. Cook garlic and lemon zest for 30 seconds.
3. Add spinach and broth.
4. Season with salt.
5. Cook for 3 minutes and serve.

Nutritional Value:

- Calories 50
- Total Fat 2.7 g
- Saturated Fat 0.4 g
- Cholesterol 0 mg
- Sodium 198 mg
- Total Carbohydrate 4.8 g
- Dietary Fiber 2.6 g
- Protein 3.5 g

Mustard & Parsley Potatoes

Preparation Time: 30 minutes; Cooking Time: 30 minutes; Servings: 1

Ingredients:

- 1 lb. potatoes, sliced
- 3 tablespoons olive oil
- Salt and pepper to taste
- 2 teaspoons dry mustard
- ¼ cup parsley, chopped

Method:

1. Preheat your oven to 450 degrees F.
2. Coat the potatoes with oil.
3. Season with salt and pepper.
4. Sprinkle with mustard and parsley.
5. Roast in the oven for 30 minutes, stirring halfway through.

Nutritional Value:

- Calories 155
- Total Fat 4 g
- Saturated Fat 0.5 g
- Cholesterol 0 mg
- Sodium 156 mg
- Total Carbohydrate 27.5 g
- Dietary Fiber 3.8 g
- Protein 3.5 g

Ginger & Miso Kale

Preparation Time: 15 minutes; Cooking Time: 0 minutes; Servings: 1

Ingredients:

- 2 tablespoons olive oil
- 2 tablespoons rice vinegar
- 1 tablespoon lime juice
- ½ teaspoon lemon zest
- 1 cups kale, chopped, steamed
- 2 teaspoons miso
- 1 clove garlic, minced
- 1 teaspoon ginger, grated
- 2 tablespoons cashews, chopped

Method:

1. Combine all the ingredients in a serving bowl.

Nutritional Value:

- Calories 86
- Total Fat 5.2 g
- Saturated Fat 0.4 g
- Cholesterol 0 mg
- Sodium 104 mg
- Total Carbohydrate 8 g
- Dietary Fiber 1.6 g
- Protein 2.8 g

Honey Balsamic Parsnips & Carrots

Preparation Time: 15 minutes; Cooking Time: 10 minutes; Servings: 1

Ingredients:

- 3 parsnips, sliced
- 1 carrots, sliced
- Water
- 1 tablespoon vegetable oil
- 1 tablespoon honey
- 2 tablespoons balsamic vinegar
- ¼ teaspoon ground nutmeg

Method:

1. Add parsnips and carrots in a pan with water over medium heat.
2. Boil for 7 minutes.
3. Drain and put the veggies back to the pan.
4. Add the oil.
5. Cook for 2 minutes.
6. In a bowl, mix the honey, vinegar and nutmeg.
7. Stir into the pan.
8. Cook for 1 minute.

Nutritional Value:

- Calories 67
- Total Fat 1.1 g
- Saturated Fat 0.2 g
- Cholesterol 0 mg
- Sodium 42 mg
- Total Carbohydrate 14 g
- Dietary Fiber 3.3 g
- Protein 0.9 g

Chapter 9: Appetizers and Snacks Recipes

Deviled Eggs with Rosemary

Preparation Time: 15 minutes; Cooking Time: 0 minutes; Servings: 1

Ingredients:

- ½ hard-boiled eggs, sliced in half
- ½ teaspoon dried rosemary
- ¼ cup mayonnaise
- 1 tablespoon mustard
- Salt to taste

Method:

1. Scoop the yolks from the hard-boiled eggs.
2. Mash the egg yolks in a bowl.
3. Stir in the rest of the ingredients.
4. Add a scoop of mixture on top of the egg whites.

Nutritional Value:

- Calories 69
- Total Fat 5.9 g
- Saturated Fat 1.3 g
- Cholesterol 95 mg
- Sodium 110 mg
- Total Carbohydrate 0.4 g
- Dietary Fiber 0.1 g
- Protein 3.2 g

Cauliflower Gnocchi with Marinara Dip

Preparation Time: 10 minutes; Cooking Time: 20 minutes; Servings: 1

Ingredients:

- 20 oz. cauliflower gnocchi
- 3 tablespoons olive oil
- ½ cup Parmesan cheese, grated
- 2 tablespoons parsley, chopped
- 1 cup marinara sauce

Method:

1. Coat cauliflower gnocchi in oil.
2. Bake in the oven at 350 degrees F for 20 minutes.
3. Sprinkle with Parmesan cheese and parsley.
4. Serve with marinara sauce.

Nutritional Value:

- Calories 159
- Total Fat 9 g
- Saturated Fat 1.9 g
- Cholesterol 4 mg
- Sodium 163 mg
- Total Carbohydrate 14 g
- Dietary Fiber 3.6 g
- Protein 3 g

Spinach Feta Dip & Crackers

Preparation Time: 10 minutes; Cooking Time: 0 minutes; Servings: 1

Ingredients:

- ¾ cup feta cheese, crumbled
- 2 oz. low-fat cream cheese
- 2 cups spinach, chopped
- 1 clove garlic, grated
- ½ cup fresh dill sprigs
- ½ cup low-fat sour cream
- Pepper to taste
- Whole-wheat crackers

Method:

1. Combine all ingredients in a food processor.
2. Pulse until smooth.
3. Serve with whole-wheat crackers.

Nutritional Value:

- Calories 75
- Total Fat 5.9 g
- Saturated Fat 3.9 g
- Cholesterol 22 mg
- Sodium 174 mg
- Total Carbohydrate 2.3 g
- Dietary Fiber 0.2 g
- Protein 3 g

Garlic Chicken Wings

Preparation Time: 15 minutes; Cooking Time: 30 minutes; Servings: 1

Ingredients:

- 2 lb. chicken wings
- ½ cup all-purpose flour
- 2 tablespoons garlic powder
- 2 teaspoons ground pepper
- 3 eggs, beaten
- 1 ½ cups panko breadcrumbs
- 1 ¼ cups Parmesan cheese, grated
- Cooking spray

Method:

1. Preheat your oven to 400 degrees F.
2. Mix flour, garlic powder and pepper in a bowl.
3. Dip chicken wings in this mixture.
4. Dip in the egg and dredge with breadcrumbs.
5. Sprinkle with Parmesan cheese.
6. Spray with oil.
7. Bake in the oven for 30 minutes.

Nutritional Value:

- Calories 221
- Total Fat 11.6 g
- Saturated Fat 3.9 g
- Cholesterol 122 mg
- Sodium 242 mg
- Total Carbohydrate 12.4 g
- Dietary Fiber 0.4 g
- Protein 16 g

Tuna Canapes

Preparation Time: 10 minutes; Cooking Time: 0 minutes; Servings: 1

Ingredients:

- 1 onion, chopped
- 5 oz. tuna flakes
- 3 oz. low-fat cream cheese
- 2 teaspoons olive oil
- 2 tablespoon chives, chopped
- ½ teaspoon liquid smoke
- ½ teaspoon Worcestershire sauce
- 1 teaspoon low-sodium Old Bay Seasoning
- 4 whole wheat crackers
- 1 cup cucumber, chopped

Method:

1. Mix all ingredients except crackers and cucumber in a bowl.
2. Spread mixture on top of crackers.
3. Top with chopped cucumber and serve.

Nutritional Value:

- Calories 112
- Total Fat 5.6 g
- Saturated Fat 2 g
- Cholesterol 21 mg
- Sodium 160 mg
- Total Carbohydrate 8.5 g
- Dietary Fiber 0.6 g
- Protein 7.4 g

Cauliflower Nachos

Preparation Time: 15 minutes; Cooking Time: 20 minutes; Servings: 1

Ingredients:

- 2 cups cauliflower florets, sliced
- 3 tablespoons avocado oil
- Salt to taste
- ¾ teaspoon chili powder
- ¾ teaspoon ground cumin
- ¾ teaspoon onion powder
- Chopped tomatoes
- Chopped avocado
- Sour cream
- Salsa

Method:

1. Coat cauliflower with oil.
2. Season with salt and spices.
3. Bake in the oven at 400 degrees F for 20 minutes.
4. Top with tomatoes and avocado.
5. Serve with sour cream and salsa.

Nutritional Value:

- Calories 487
- Total Fat 28 g
- Saturated Fat 6.6 g
- Cholesterol 79 mg
- Sodium 484 mg
- Total Carbohydrate 27 g
- Dietary Fiber 11 g
- Protein 35 g

Goat Cheese Crostini

Preparation Time: 15 minutes; Cooking Time: 25 minutes; Servings: 1

Ingredients:

- ¼ cup honey
- 1 oz. figs, diced
- ¼ cup orange juice
- ¼ cup lemon juice
- 1 teaspoon fresh rosemary, minced
- 3 tablespoons water
- Salt and pepper to taste
- 2 whole-wheat baguette
- 1 tablespoon olive oil
- 6 oz. goat cheese

Method:

1. Mix honey, figs, orange juice, lemon juice, rosemary, water, salt and pepper in a pan over medium heat.
2. Simmer for 15 minutes.
3. Spread mixture on top of baguette slices.
4. Add to a baking pan.
5. Bake in the oven at 375 degrees F for 10 minutes.
6. Top with goat cheese and serve.

Nutritional Value:

- Calories 137
- Total Fat 3.6 g
- Saturated Fat 1.8 g
- Cholesterol 5 mg
- Sodium 183 mg
- Total Carbohydrate 22.9 g
- Dietary Fiber 1 g
- Protein 4 g

Cheesy Apple Bites

Preparation Time: 10 minutes; Cooking Time: 10 minutes; Servings: 1

Ingredients:

- Cooking spray
- 1 pie crust
- ¼ cup apple butter
- ½ cup cheddar cheese, shredded
- 1 thin apple slices

Method:

1. Preheat your oven to 450 degrees F.
2. Spray your muffin pan with oil.
3. Cut circles on the dough using a cookie cutter.
4. Press the circles into muffin cups.
5. Bake for 5 minutes.
6. Top with the apple butter, cheese and apple slices.
7. Bake for another 5 minutes.
8. Let cool and serve warm.

Nutritional Value:

- Calories 51
- Total Fat 2.9 g
- Saturated Fat 1.2 g
- Cholesterol 0 mg
- Sodium 49 mg
- Total Carbohydrate 5.5 g
- Dietary Fiber 0.2 g
- Protein 0.8 g

Roasted Vegetable Spread

Preparation Time: 20 minutes; Cooking Time: 40 minutes; Servings: 1

Ingredients:

- 2 red bell peppers, sliced in half
- 1 lb. tomatoes, sliced into wedges
- 3 cloves garlic, peeled
- 1 onion, sliced in wedges
- 2 tablespoons olive oil
- Salt and pepper to taste
- 2 tablespoons balsamic vinegar
- 2 teaspoons fresh thyme, chopped
- ¼ cup fresh basil, chopped

Method:

1. Preheat your oven to 425 degrees F.
2. Toss the vegetables in olive oil and season with salt and pepper.
3. Roast in the oven for 40 minutes.
4. Transfer to a food processor.
5. Stir in the rest of the ingredients.

Nutritional Value:

- Calories 57
- Total Fat 3.3 g
- Saturated Fat 0.4 g
- Cholesterol 0 mg
- Sodium 113 mg
- Total Carbohydrate 6.5 g
- Dietary Fiber 1.5 g
- Protein 1.1 g

Turkey Nachos

Preparation Time: 30 minutes; Cooking Time: 4 hours; Servings: 1

Ingredients:

- 1 ½ lb. turkey breast fillet
- Pepper to taste
- 2 tablespoons lime juice
- 2 tablespoons chili powder
- 1 teaspoon ground cumin
- 1 tablespoon honey
- 3 cloves garlic, minced
- 1 ½ cups pico de gallo
- ½ cup fresh cilantro, chopped
- 1 oz. baked tortilla chips
- 2 oz. Mexican cheese, crumbled

Method:

1. Sprinkle turkey with pepper.
2. Place in a slow cooker.
3. Stir in the rest of the ingredients except chips and cheese.
4. Cover the pot and cook on low for 4 hours.
5. Shred the turkey.
6. Return to the pot and stir.
7. Place chips in a serving plate.
8. Sprinkle shredded turkey mixture on top.
9. Top with cheese.

Nutritional Value:

- Calories 297
- Total Fat 9 g
- Saturated Fat 2 g
- Cholesterol 0 mg
- Sodium 600 mg
- Total Carbohydrate 26 g
- Dietary Fiber 5 g
- Protein 29 g

Stuffed Mushrooms

Preparation Time: 15 minutes; Cooking Time: 15 minutes; Servings: 1

Ingredients:

- Cooking spray
- 1 mushrooms buttons
- Salt and pepper to taste
- ¼ cup whole-wheat breadcrumbs
- 4 oz. cream cheese
- 2 tablespoons parsley, chopped

Method:

1. Spray mushrooms with oil and season with salt and pepper.
2. Mix breadcrumbs, cream cheese and parsley in a bowl.
3. Stuff the mixture into the mushrooms.
4. Bake in the oven at 350 degrees F for 15 minutes.

Nutritional Value:

- Calories 75
- Total Fat 4 g
- Saturated Fat 2 g
- Cholesterol 0 mg
- Sodium 184 mg
- Total Carbohydrate 7 g
- Dietary Fiber 1 g
- Protein 4 g

Antipasto Skewers

Preparation Time: 15 minutes; Cooking Time: 0 minutes; Servings: 1

Ingredients:

- 6 red bell pepper, sliced
- 1 slices salami, sliced in half and cooked
- 2 basil leaves
- 2 black olives
- 1 teaspoon chopped rosemary
- 2 teaspoons white wine vinegar
- 3 teaspoons olive oil

Method:

1. Thread red bell pepper, salami, basil leaves and olives onto skewers.
2. In a bowl, mix rosemary, vinegar and oil.
3. Drizzle over the skewers and serve.

Nutritional Value:

- Calories 96
- Total Fat 7 g
- Saturated Fat 2 g
- Cholesterol 0 mg
- Sodium 205 mg
- Total Carbohydrate 6 g
- Dietary Fiber 1 g
- Protein 3 g

Chapter 10: Drinks Recipes

Strawberry Smoothie With Almonds & Tofu

Preparation Time: 5 minutes; Cooking Time: 0 minutes; Servings: 1

Ingredients:

- 1 cup coconut milk
- 2 tablespoons honey
- 5 strawberries, sliced
- ½ cup silken tofu

Method:

1. Pour milk and honey into a blender.
2. Stir in strawberries and tofu.
3. Process until smooth.

Nutritional Value:

- Calories 171
- Total Fat 3.3 g
- Saturated Fat 0 g
- Cholesterol 0 mg
- Sodium 105 mg
- Total Carbohydrate 20 g
- Dietary Fiber 3 g
- Protein 4.6 g

Green Tea with Honey

Preparation Time: 15 minutes; Cooking Time: 20 minutes; Serving: 1

Ingredients:

- 1 lemon peel
- 1 orange peel
- 1 cup hot water
- 1 green tea bag
- 1 teaspoon honey
- 1 lemon slice

Method:

1. Combine fruit peels and hot water in a pan over medium heat.
2. Bring to a boil.
3. Reduce heat and simmer for 10 minutes.
4. Discard fruit peels.
5. Add tea bag to the pot.
6. Turn off heat.
7. Simmer for 5 minutes.
8. Pour mixture into a tea cup.
9. Stir in honey and garnish with lemon slice.

Nutritional Value:

- Calories 16
- Total Fat 0 g
- Saturated Fat 0 g
- Cholesterol 0 mg
- Sodium 8 mg
- Total Carbohydrate 5 g
- Dietary Fiber 0.6 g
- Protein 0.2 g

Orange Lemon Juice

Preparation Time: 5 minutes; Cooking Time: 0 minutes; Serving: 1

Ingredients:

- 1 orange, sliced into 2
- 1 lemon, sliced into 2
- 1 tablespoon honey
- 2 glasses water

Method:

1. Use a juicer to squeeze juice from orange and lemon.
2. Transfer to drinking glasses.
3. Stir in honey.
4. Pour in water.
5. Mix.
6. Chill before serving.

Nutritional Value:

- Calories 80
- Total Fat 5 g
- Saturated Fat 0 g
- Cholesterol 0 mg
- Sodium 12 mg
- Total Carbohydrate 8 g
- Dietary Fiber 3 g
- Protein 20 g

Pineapple & Strawberry Smoothie

Preparation Time: 10 minutes; Cooking Time: 0 minutes; Serving: 1

Ingredients:

- 1 cup strawberries
- 1 cup pineapple, chopped
- ¾ cup almond milk
- 1 tablespoon almond butter

Method:

1. Add all ingredients to a blender.
2. Blend until smooth.
3. Add more almond milk until it reaches your desired consistency.
4. Chill before serving.

Nutritional Value:

- Calories 255
- Total Fat 11.1 g
- Saturated Fat 1.1 g
- Cholesterol 0 mg
- Sodium 168 mg
- Total Carbohydrate 39 g
- Dietary Fiber 7.8 g
- Protein 5.6 g

Sage Tea

Preparation Time: 10 minutes; Cooking Time: 0 minutes; Serving: 1

Ingredients:

- 10 sage leaves
- 1 cup hot water
- 1 teaspoon honey
- 1 teaspoon lemon juice

Method:

1. Steep the sage leaves in hot water for 5 to 10 minutes.
2. Discard sage leaves.
3. Pour in lemon juice.
4. Stir in honey.
5. Serve while warm.

Nutritional Value:

- Calories 22
- Total Fat 0 g
- Saturated Fat 0 g
- Cholesterol 0 mg
- Sodium 7 mg
- Total Carbohydrate 6.1 g
- Dietary Fiber 1 g
- Protein 2 g

Berry Smoothie With Mint

Preparation Time: 5 minutes; Cooking Time: 0 minutes; Servings: 1

Ingredients:

- ¼ cup orange juice
- ½ cup blueberries
- ½ cup blackberries
- 1 cup reduced-fat plain kefir
- 1 tablespoon honey
- 1 tablespoons fresh mint leaves

Method:

1. Add all the ingredients to a blender.
2. Blend until smooth.

Nutritional Value:

- Calories 137
- Total Fat 1 g
- Saturated Fat 1 g
- Cholesterol 5 mg
- Sodium 64 mg
- Total Carbohydrate 27 g
- Dietary Fiber 4 g
- Protein 6 g

Mint Melonade

Preparation Time: 1 hour and 15 minutes; Cooking Time: 0 minutes; Servings: 1

Ingredients:

- ½ cup lime juice
- 3 lb. honeydew melon, sliced into cubes
- 1 mint leaves, chopped and divided
- 1 cups soda water

Method:

1. Process lime juice, melon and half of mint leaves in a blender.
2. Transfer to a container and refrigerate for 1 hour.
3. Pour into serving glasses.
4. Pour soda water on top and serve.

Nutritional Value:

- Calories 60
- Total Fat 0.2 g
- Saturated Fat 0.1 g
- Cholesterol 0 mg
- Sodium 45 mg
- Total Carbohydrate 15.4 g
- Dietary Fiber 1.3 g
- Protein 0.9 g

Green Smoothie

Preparation Time: 10 minutes; Cooking Time: 0 minutes; Serving: 1

Ingredients:

- 1 cup vanilla almond milk (unsweetened)
- ¼ ripe avocado, chopped
- 1 cup kale, chopped
- 1 banana
- 2 teaspoons honey
- 1 tablespoon chia seeds
- 1 cup ice cubes

Method:

1. Combine all the ingredients in a blender.
2. Process until creamy.

Nutritional Value:

- Calories 343
- Total Fat 14.2 g
- Saturated Fat 1.6 g
- Cholesterol 0 mg
- Sodium 199 mg
- Total Carbohydrate 54.7 g
- Dietary Fiber 12.1 g
- Protein 5.9 g

Hawaiian Smoothie

Preparation Time: 10 minutes; Cooking Time: 0 minutes; Servings: 1

Ingredients:

- ½ cup papaya, sliced into cubes
- 1 cup pineapple chunks
- 1 tablespoon lemon juice
- ¼ cup guava nectar
- ½ cup crushed ice

Method:

1. Add the fruits to a blender.
2. Pulse until chopped.
3. Stir in the juice, nectar and ice.
4. Process until smooth.

Nutritional Value:

- Calories 86
- Total Fat 0.2 g
- Saturated Fat 0.1 g
- Cholesterol 0 mg
- Sodium 7 mg
- Total Carbohydrate 22.4 g
- Dietary Fiber 2 g
- Protein 0.7 g

Mango Smoothie with Yogurt

Preparation Time: 5 minutes; Cooking Time: 0 minutes; Servings: 1

Ingredients:

- 1 cup mango, chopped
- ½ cup yogurt
- ⅓ cup peach sorbet
- ¼ cup orange juice

Method:

1. Add mango to a blender.
2. Pulse until finely chopped.
3. Stir in the rest of the ingredients.
4. Blend until smooth.
5. Chill before serving.

Nutritional Value:

- Calories 163
- Total Fat 0.5 g
- Saturated Fat 0.2 g
- Cholesterol 1 mg
- Sodium 43 mg
- Total Carbohydrate 37.3 g
- Dietary Fiber 1.5 g
- Protein 4 g

Vegan Fruit Smoothie

Preparation Time: 5 minutes; Cooking Time: 0 minutes; Servings: 1

Ingredients:

- ¾ cup orange juice
- ½ cup peaches
- ¼ cup silken tofu
- 1 tablespoon honey

Method:

1. Mix all the ingredients in a blender.
2. Blend until smooth.
3. Chill before serving.

Nutritional Value:

- Calories 166
- Total Fat 2.9 g
- Saturated Fat 0.1 g
- Cholesterol 0 mg
- Sodium 27 mg
- Total Carbohydrate 31 g
- Dietary Fiber 3.3 g
- Protein 5.8 g

Watermelon & Turmeric Smoothie

Preparation Time: 10 minutes; Cooking Time: 0 minutes; Servings: 1

Ingredients:

- 1 tablespoons lemon juice
- 1 cups watermelon, sliced into cubes
- 1 teaspoons honey
- 1 teaspoon ginger, minced
- 1 teaspoon ground turmeric
- ½ cup water

Method:

1. Combine all the ingredients in a blender.
2. Process until pureed.
3. Chill before serving.

Nutritional Value:

- Calories 169
- Total Fat 2.9 g
- Saturated Fat 2.1 g
- Cholesterol 0 mg
- Sodium 7 mg
- Total Carbohydrate 38.5 g
- Dietary Fiber 1.8 g
- Protein 2.3 g

Chapter 11: Desserts Recipes

Peanut Butter Cups

Preparation Time: 3 hours and 15 minutes; Cooking Time: 10 minutes; Servings: 1

Ingredients:

- 1 packet plain gelatin
- ¼ cup sugar substitute
- 2 cups nonfat cream
- ½ teaspoon vanilla
- ¼ cup low-fat peanut butter
- 2 tablespoons unsalted peanuts, chopped

Method:

1. Mix gelatin, sugar substitute and cream in a pan.
2. Let sit for 5 minutes.
3. Place over medium heat and cook until gelatin has been dissolved.
4. Stir in vanilla and peanut butter.
5. Pour into custard cups. Chill for 3 hours.
6. Top with the peanuts and serve.

Nutritional Value:

- Calories 171
- Total Fat 5.6 g
- Saturated Fat 1.1 g
- Cholesterol 0 mg
- Sodium 172 mg
- Total Carbohydrate 21 g
- Dietary Fiber 0.6 g
- Protein 6.8 g

Vanilla Pudding Pops

Preparation Time: 1 hour and 10 minutes; Cooking Time: 0 minutes; Servings: 1

Ingredients:

- 1 pack nonfat and sugar free vanilla pudding mix
- 2 cups nonfat milk
- 1 teaspoon vanilla
- 1 cup light whipped dessert topping

Method:

1. Mix all the ingredients in a bowl.
2. Pour into popsicle molds.
3. Freeze for 1 hour.

Nutritional Value:

- Calories 72
- Total Fat 1.1 g
- Saturated Fat 1 g
- Cholesterol 1 mg
- Sodium 168 mg
- Total Carbohydrate 13.4 g
- Dietary Fiber 0.4 g
- Protein 2.2 g

Brûléed Oranges

Preparation Time: 10 minutes; Cooking Time: 5 minutes; Servings: 1

Ingredients:

- 1 oranges, sliced into segments
- 1 teaspoon ground cardamom
- 1.5 teaspoons brown sugar
- 1 cup nonfat Greek yogurt

Method:

1. Preheat your broiler.
2. Arrange orange slices in a baking pan.
3. In a bowl, mix the cardamom and sugar.
4. Sprinkle mixture on top of the oranges. Broil for 5 minutes.
5. Serve oranges with yogurt.

Nutritional Value:

- Calories 168
- Total Fat 4.2 g
- Saturated Fat 1.5 g
- Cholesterol 8 mg
- Sodium 25 mg
- Total Carbohydrate 26.9 g
- Dietary Fiber 2.8 g
- Protein 6.8 g

Strawberry & Watermelon Pops

Preparation Time: 15 minutes; Cooking Time: 0 minutes; Servings: 1

Ingredients:

- 2 cups watermelon, chopped
- 1 cup strawberries, chopped
- 2 tablespoons sugar substitute
- ¼ cup lime juice
- Pinch salt

Method:

1. Combine all the ingredients in a food processor.
2. Blend until smooth.
3. Pour mixture into popsicle molds.
4. Freeze for 6 hours.

Nutritional Value:

- Calories 57
- Total Fat 0.3 g
- Saturated Fat 0 g
- Cholesterol 0 mg
- Sodium 51 mg
- Total Carbohydrate 14.5 g
- Dietary Fiber 1.6 g
- Protein 0.8 g

Strawberry & Mango Ice Cream

Preparation Time: 10 minutes; Cooking Time: 0 minutes; Servings: 1

Ingredients:

- 2 oz. strawberries, sliced
- 3 oz. mango, sliced into cubes
- 1 tablespoon lime juice

Method:

1. Add all ingredients in a food processor.
2. Pulse for 2 minutes.
3. Chill before serving.

Nutritional Value:

- Calories 70
- Total Fat 0.5 g
- Saturated Fat 0.1 g
- Cholesterol 0 mg
- Sodium 1 mg
- Total Carbohydrate 17.4 g
- Dietary Fiber 2.5 g
- Protein 1.1 g

Spiced Apples

Preparation Time: 10 minutes; Cooking Time: 0 minutes; Servings: 1

Ingredients:

- 1 apples, sliced thinly
- ¼ cup water
- ½ teaspoon ground cinnamon
- ⅛ teaspoon ground nutmeg
- 2 tablespoons honey

Method:

1. Combine all the ingredients except honey in a pan over medium heat.
2. Bring to a boil.
3. Reduce heat and simmer for 3 minutes.
4. Drizzle with honey before serving.

Nutritional Value:

- Calories 101
- Total Fat 0.3 g
- Saturated Fat 0.1 g
- Cholesterol 0 mg
- Sodium 2 mg
- Total Carbohydrate 26.9 g
- Dietary Fiber 3.8 g
- Protein 0.4 g

Choco Chip Balls

Preparation Time: 1 hour and 30 minutes; Cooking Time: 0 minutes; Servings: 1

Ingredients:

- ½ cup almond butter
- 2 oz. chickpeas, rinsed and drained
- 1 teaspoon vanilla extract
- ¼ cup sugar substitute
- Pinch salt
- ¼ cup dark chocolate chips

Method:

1. Add all ingredients except chocolate chips in a food processor.
2. Pulse until smooth.
3. Transfer to a bowl.
4. Add chocolate chips.
5. Mix well.
6. Form balls from the mixture.
7. Freeze for 1 hour.

Nutritional Value:

- Calories 161
- Total Fat 8.6 g
- Saturated Fat 2.1 g
- Cholesterol 0 mg
- Sodium 145 mg
- Total Carbohydrate 16 g
- Dietary Fiber 2.4 g
- Protein 4.5 g

Pumpkin & Banana Ice Cream

Preparation Time: 10 minutes; Cooking Time: 0 minutes; Servings: 1

Ingredients:

- 2 oz. pumpkin puree
- 4 bananas, sliced and frozen
- 1 teaspoon pumpkin pie spice
- Chopped pecans

Method:

1. Add pumpkin puree, bananas and pumpkin pie spice in a food processor.
2. Pulse until smooth.
3. Chill in the refrigerator.
4. Garnish with pecans.

Nutritional Value:

- Calories 71
- Total Fat 0.4 g
- Saturated Fat 0.2 g
- Cholesterol 0.2 mg
- Sodium 3 mg
- Total Carbohydrate 18 g
- Dietary Fiber 3.1 g
- Protein 1.2 g

Ice Cream Brownie Cake

Preparation Time: 10 hours; Cooking Time: 25 minutes; Servings: 1

Ingredients:

- Cooking spray
- 1 oz. no-sugar brownie mix
- ¼ cup oil
- 2 egg whites
- 3 tablespoons water
- 2 cups sugar-free ice cream

Method:

1. Preheat your oven to 325 degrees F.
2. Spray your baking pan with oil.
3. Mix brownie mix, oil, egg whites and water in a bowl.
4. Pour into the baking pan.
5. Bake for 25 minutes.
6. Let cool.
7. Freeze brownie for 2 hours.
8. Spread ice cream over the brownie.
9. Freeze for 8 hours.

Nutritional Value:

- Calories 198
- Total Fat 10 g
- Saturated Fat 1 g
- Cholesterol 3 mg
- Sodium 118 mg
- Total Carbohydrate 33 g
- Dietary Fiber 4 g
- Protein 3 g

Fruit Kebabs

Preparation Time: 20 minutes; Cooking Time: 0 minutes; Servings: 1

Ingredients:

- 3 apples, sliced
- 1 ½ lb. watermelon, sliced
- ¾ cup blueberries
- ¼ cup orange juice

Method:

1. Thread fruit slices onto skewers.
2. Drizzle with orange juice and serve.

Nutritional Value:

- Calories 52
- Total Fat 0.2 g
- Saturated Fat 0 g
- Cholesterol 0 mg
- Sodium 1 mg
- Total Carbohydrate 13.5 g
- Dietary Fiber 1.8 g
- Protein 0.6 g

Apricot Pizza

Preparation Time: 10 minutes; Cooking Time: 5 minutes; Servings: 1

Ingredients:

- 1 tablespoon apricot preserves (unsweetened)
- 2 tablespoons low-fat cream cheese
- 1 artisan pizza flatbread
- 1 kiwi, sliced thinly
- 1 apricot, sliced thinly
- 2 tablespoons honey

Method:

1. In a bowl, mix apricot preserves and cream cheese.
2. Spread mixture on top of the flatbread.
3. Top with the fruit slices.
4. Grill for 3 to 4 minutes.
5. Drizzle with honey.

Nutritional Value:

- Calories 127
- Total Fat 3.3 g
- Saturated Fat 0.9 g
- Cholesterol 5 mg
- Sodium 89 mg
- Total Carbohydrate 22.9 g
- Dietary Fiber 2 g
- Protein 3.3 g

Roasted Mango

Preparation Time: 10 minutes; Cooking Time: 10 minutes; Servings: 1

Ingredients:

- 2 mangoes, sliced
- 2 teaspoons crystallized ginger, chopped
- 2 teaspoons orange zest
- 2 tablespoons coconut flakes (unsweetened)

Method:

1. Preheat your oven to 350 degrees F.
2. Add mango slices in custard cups.
3. Top with the ginger, orange zest and coconut flakes.
4. Bake in the oven for 10 minutes.

Nutritional Value:

- Calories 89
- Total Fat 1.5 g
- Saturated Fat 1.3 g
- Cholesterol 0 mg
- Sodium 14 mg
- Total Carbohydrate 20 g
- Dietary Fiber 2.2 g
- Protein 0.8 g

Conclusion

If you are one of the people struggling with diabetes, the biggest obstacle to meal preparation can be life. Since staring into the refrigerator waiting for inspiration isn't an option, having a simple, delicious, and practical diabetic cookbook like the Diabetic Cookbook for One, is essential to managing your condition.

With clear recipes and guidance, this dedicated diabetic cookbook will help you prepare balanced, full meals that will feed your whole family. Cooking becomes more convenient, mealtime becomes more integrated, and all with just a few kitchen tools and basic cooking techniques—a truly inclusive diabetic cookbook.